A BETTER COUNTRY

Cindy Wu's workbook is practical, biblical, and incredibly relevant in today's climate of misunderstanding. Followers of Jesus will find this workbook inspiring as they seek to befriend the refugees in our midst in an effort to "act justly, love mercy and walk humbly with our God."

A-K Besancon, MS
co-founder, Houston Welcomes Refugees

Over several years, I have watched Cindy Wu read, study, listen to, feel personally, and write about refugees and their situations in the United States. She has done so with deep compassion joined together with objective realism. This most timely workbook should be widely read and used in churches across our land.

Dean Borgman, MA
senior professor of youth ministries and social ethics, Gordon-Conwell Theological Seminary

Every Christian, wishing to find the balance between security and compassion should work through *A Better Country*. Wu serves the church by presenting an excellent foundation for understanding refugee history, journey, and advocacy. This timely workbook presents facts to alleviate unnecessary fears in these important days.

David Daniels, DMin
lead pastor, Pantego Bible Church

A wonderful new book on helping refugees and immigrants is now available. Cindy M. Wu has produced a book titled, *A Better Country: Embracing the Refugees in Our Midst*. Ms. Wu lives in Houston, America's most ethnically diverse city, and practices the kind of hospitality she espouses. Out of her own experience and interest, she offers a workbook to help the reader learn about refugees and to embrace the challenge of offering them hospitality. I envision a Sunday school class or home group using this valuable resource in a group study. Ms. Wu artfully combines up-to-date statistics on displaced persons, refugee stories, and words of challenge for those who wish to serve others. She refers to Mariane from Rwanda in the introduction and then quotes her in the book's conclusion: "People have many freedoms here (USA) and hard work pays off. Close the door behind you and open another one. You don't have to live in between doors." That is the challenge Cindy Wu extends to her readers. Be a door-opener for the world's refugee peoples wherever you find them.

Richard L. Haney, PhD
executive director, Frontier Fellowship

A Better Country is a book for such a time as this. More than 65 million people in the world have been forced to flee their homes and are seeking a better life. Cindy Wu provides a solid biblical, moral, and historical basis for welcoming refugees into our country and into our communities. *A Better Country* is a very practical guide for both churches and individuals, filled with resources and suggestions for how Christians can live out the biblical call to welcome the stranger.

David Husby, MDiv
director, Covenant World Relief

Cindy Wu's new book is a remarkable fusion of facts, personal experience, and biblical reflection on how Christians should treat migrants and strangers. As the West increasingly closes its heart, mind, and homelands to the rest of the world, this is a timely prophetic call to the church to follow Jesus' example and welcome the stranger. As a bonus, Wu's approach is highly practical, providing a much-needed tool for churches and small groups to study and to act.

Todd M. Johnson, PhD
director, Center for the Study of Global Christianity
associate professor of global Christianity, Gordon-Conwell Theological Seminary

At a time when the arrival of refugees is mired in misinformation and fear, Cindy Wu has created a fantastic, timely resource in *A Better Country*. With insightful analysis, biblical wisdom, and clear applications, this is a superb resource for Christians searching for a deeper understanding of refugees.

Matthew Soerens, MS
US director of church mobilization, World Relief

A BETTER

EMBRACING THE REFUGEES IN OUR MIDST

COUNTRY

CINDY M. WU

WILLIAM CAREY
LIBRARY

Cover Art: "May angels protect you on your journey to safety" by Jacqueline Kramer

Published by William Carey Library
Pasadena, CA 91104 | www.missionbooks.org

Joanne Liang, graphic design

William Carey Library is a ministry of
Frontier Ventures
Pasadena, CA | www.frontierventures.org

Printed in the United States of America
21 20 19 18 17   5 4 3 2 1 BP300

Library of Congress Cataloging-in-Publication Data

Names: Wu, Cindy M., author.
Title: A better country : embracing the refugees in our midst / Cindy M. Wu.
Description: Pasadena, CA : William Carey Library, [2017] | Includes
   bibliographical references.
Identifiers: LCCN 2017003563| ISBN 9780878085460 (pbk.) | ISBN 0878085467
   (pbk.)
Subjects: LCSH: Church work with refugees. | Church work with immigrants.
Classification: LCC BV4466 .W8 2017 | DDC 261.8/328--dc23 LC record available at
https://lccn.loc.gov/2017003563

CONTENTS

TABLES

GRAPHS

PREFACE

In 2009 I took a seminary course that would change the direction of my ministry calling. I was a student at Gordon-Conwell Theological Seminary in South Hamilton, Massachusetts, just beginning my degree. The course, titled "Biblical Global Justice," was taught by Dean Borgman, a spry, white-haired Episcopal priest with a passion for justice and for youth.

Professor Borgman's class was eye-opening and uncomfortable, in a sanctifying way. I had always cared about social issues, but had never explored the theological foundations for justice. By then I had already lived in several countries around the world—and among the poor in one of them—and yet I was still so sheltered from some of the greatest suffering and injustice on earth. And I was limited not just in my experiences, but also in any deeper reflection on the subject. Borgman's class challenged me to think about justice on a larger scale.

The following semester, I took a class at Boston University, "Christianity in Asia, Africa, and Latin America," with church historian Dr. Dana Robert. One of our required readings for the course was *Blood Brothers*, the memoir of Elias Chacour, a Palestinian Christian.[1] Chacour grew up in Galilee in a peaceful co-existence with Jewish neighbors. The United Nations partition of Mandatory Palestine in 1947 turned Palestinian land over to Zionists, leading to civil war and resulting in death or displacement for over one million Palestinians. Chacour's village was obliterated; his family fled. Chacour went on to study in Europe, and later in life, as the Israeli-Palestinian conflict raged on in his homeland, he found his high calling: to be a peacemaker between the two groups of "blood brothers."

I confess that before reading *Blood Brothers*, I had never wondered whether there were Christians in Palestine. I had never given thought to the experience of the Palestinians who had been forced into exile. I had only pictured Palestinians as armed, turbaned PLO (Palestinian Liberation Organization) terrorists, based off what I had seen on the news. I was confronted with my prejudice and one-sided thinking.

---

1. Elias Chacour, with David Hazard, *Blood Brothers: The Dramatic Story of a Palestinian Christian Working for Peace in Israel* (Grand Rapids: Chosen Books, 2003).

During seminary, God grew in me a concern for social justice in both local and global contexts. At the time, my husband and I felt called to ministry in the States, so the question for me, then, was how to blend my passion for global missions and social justice while staying in our home country.

One day while sitting at my desk at the seminary library, God gave me clarity: refugees. My parents' immigrant background had already given me a heart for newcomers in America. And my combined interests in the nations and social justice could converge in advocating for and caring for refugees. But first I had to learn more.

I started volunteering with a ministry to refugees in the Boston area. I also asked Dean Borgman if he would supervise a self-designed independent study on the global refugee crisis, and he graciously agreed. That study eventually became the basis for my graduation project. I then asked Dr. Todd Johnson, Director of the Center for the Study of Global Christianity, to advise my project, which, many edits later, is this workbook you are holding in your hands.

After graduation my family returned to our hometown of Houston, TX, and my husband and I, along with our three kids, have been volunteering with refugees here for the past five years, in America's current #1 resettlement city. We assist with donations for newcomers moving into their apartments, we "adopt" refugee families, and I contribute to World Refugee Day Houston as a writer and event volunteer.

One of the highlights of my friendship with refugees is my Iraqi friend, Abeer. Abeer frequently calls me her "sister." She, an Orthodox Christian, and I have so little in common on the surface, and yet we have been able to receive and give love to one another through simple acts of hospitality and assistance. I help her navigate the challenges of re-establishing life in a new city; she inspires me by her love and sacrifice for her family. She has also introduced me to some pretty tasty food!

I am grateful to live in a city that welcomes refugees. I continue to be amazed by the resilience, perseverance, and determination of the refugees in my community. My Christian faith compels me to advocate for and care for the refugees around me. Won't you join me?

INTRODUCTION

The night Mariane Uwimana[2] left her home in Rwanda in 1994, she didn't know where she was going. She was eight months pregnant with her second child and afraid for her life. A civil war between the two majority ethnic groups in Rwanda—the Hutus and the Tutsis—resulted in one of the worst genocides in modern history. Neighbor slaughtered neighbor, friend betrayed friend. The country was awash in a bloodbath, and masses of people were fleeing the country, many on foot. With only the clothes on their backs, Mariane and her husband walked from their home, past piles of massacred bodies lining the roads, toward uncertainty.

They made their way to a refugee camp in Zaire (now Democratic Republic of the Congo). Poverty and illness permeated the place; they encountered suffering every direction they turned. The Uwimanas sought relief. From the refugee camp they moved to Burkina Faso, where Mariane gave birth to their second son only two weeks after arrival. Life there was tough, but bearable. After a few months, both Mariane and her husband found jobs.

Although grateful to have preserved her life, in the struggle to survive Mariane felt like she had "lost herself." She had already lost all her earthly possessions, and now she was losing her identity. She became a shadow of who she was. Educated, capable, and strong, Mariane was now at the mercy of others. The Uwimanas applied to the United Nations for refugee resettlement, hoping for a better outlook. After three years in Burkina Faso, they were finally approved for resettlement in the United States.

On average, twenty-four persons were forced to flee their homes every minute of 2015. That's more than 34,000 people every day, or 12.4 million newly displaced people in 2015 alone—or as many people as live in Illinois—joining the tens of millions like them who have left behind home, livelihood, and life as they knew it. As of this writing,

---

2. Personal interview with author. Name changed for privacy.

there are an estimated 65.3 million forcibly displaced persons in the world, 21.3 million of whom have left their countries of origin and are classified as "refugees."[3] These numbers are staggering.

DISPLACE: to displace means to force (someone) to leave their home, typically because of war, persecution, or natural disaster.

For decades the United States has resettled refugees. Refugees live in every state in the US, from major metroplexes to small towns. Some people welcome this, but some do not. Americans have long been conflicted over how to view refugees, how to vet them, how to integrate them into society . . . whether they belong here at all. And American Christians find themselves politically and ethically divided on this controversial and often volatile subject.

The Bible commands charity and hospitality to strangers and sojourners, and care for the distraught and downtrodden, people like refugees. Hence people who follow Jesus and take his Word seriously have a special mandate to address the needs of refugees. But the complexities of the refugee system and concerns over national security often overshadow the call to justice and mercy. In fact some Christians are calling for our country to close our doors to immigrants and refugees.

Regardless of where one stands on immigration reform, Americans must acknowledge that they have a role to play in the solution to the refugee crisis, the primary humanitarian issue of our day. We cannot and must not isolate ourselves from this global phenomenon. As the debate on immigration intensifies, how will Christians respond to this growing population from every tribe and tongue? How can we do a better job embracing newcomers? How can we be better at loving mercy and doing justice with regard to refugees? How can we *be* a better country for refugees?

HOW TO USE THIS WORKBOOK

This study aims to help Christians—specifically Christians in the United States—think theologically and practically about the global refugee crisis. The workbook is divided into seven lessons, including a Personal Action Plan as your concluding application. You can do the lessons on your own or in a group setting. You will probably find the greatest benefit by working through the workbook with others and hearing other perspectives.

---

3. United Nations High Commissioner for Refugees, *Global Trends Report 2015*, www.unhcr.org/576408cd7.pdf. Definitions for the different classifications of migrants will be provided in Chapter 1.

If doing this in a group, designate one person to facilitate or lead, and remember to follow principles of group discussion. Refugees are a "hot" topic right now. Keep the temperature of your discussion mild by respecting some basic principles of group discussion (see sidebar).

Each lesson has instructional content intermingled with reflection questions so that you are processing as you learn. It is my hope that this study will get you in action to respond to the refugee crisis. My prayer for you is that you will develop a heart to welcome refugees with compassion and dignity in Jesus' name.

DO:
- Be slow to speak, quick to listen.
- Allow everyone to speak their mind.
- Be respectful when someone disagrees with your opinion.

DO NOT:
- Monopolize the conversation.
- Judge someone's faith if they come to conclusions different from yours.
- Make personal attacks if someone disagrees with you.

CHAPTER 1
GLOBAL PEOPLE, GLOBAL PROBLEMS

We are all living in one big town.
MARY PIPHER

BEFORE WE BEGIN

In this chapter you will learn about the modern day global refugee crisis. We will make distinctions between the different types of migrants and learn how global protection for refugees got started.

What are the first three words or images that pop into your mind when you hear the word "refugee"?

What fears or unknowns come to mind when you think about refugees resettling in the US?

Look around your home. Chances are your clothes, food, furniture, and appliances come from all around the world. This might be something you now take for granted. Goods that once took weeks to arrive by slow ship can be ordered online and delivered to your home within days. You can access television and radio programming in multiple languages from your living room sofa without paying an extra dime.

Look around our country's major cities. You see crowds in all colors. You can drive down Main Street and find restaurants serving cuisine from distant lands.

There is nothing remarkable about this anymore.

Globalization has linked the peoples of the globe to one another in unprecedented ways. On the one hand, living in a globalized world creates a sense of connectedness and closeness. Globalization has the potential to enhance development and reduce inequality. On the other hand, a global economy can cause social, political, and economic upheaval. Problems that face a part of the world far away now have nearby impact.

Today we are facing a crisis with worldwide reverberations—the global refugee crisis. In 2015 there were an estimated 65.3 million forcibly displaced persons in the world. That's roughly the entire populations of California and Texas! That number ranks the current refugee crisis as the worst humanitarian crisis since World War II, surpassing what was then the largest mass human displacement in history.

Why are so many people displaced today? Several factors contribute:

- Economic deprivation: Migrants are forced by poverty and lack of development to seek better economic opportunity as a means of basic survival.
- Repression: Political instability and corruption, often in the form of totalitarian regimes, deny citizens human rights.
- Environment: Environmental degradation or natural disasters destroy the land. Political dynamics often worsen the impact of natural disasters.
- Violence: War and civil unrest can force someone to flee for fear of his physical safety.
- Persecution: Discrimination or ill-treatment based on a person's identity, religion, or affiliation often turns into a threat on someone's life.

In our connected world, a forced migration crisis that takes place in one part of the world will inevitably impact other parts of the world. A crisis of this scale requires a global, concerted response. In 1950, a global refugee protection regime was created to provide that response.

Write down the name of one country that is currently producing refugees, perhaps some place you've heard about in the news. What do you know about the cause of the refugee outflow?

REFUGEE AND ASYLUM REGIME IN THE TWENTIETH CENTURY

The first international effort for refugees began in 1921 under the League of Nations with the collaboration of international humanitarian organizations. In order to address the large-scale refugee populations produced by World War II, the Office of the United Nations High Commissioner for Refugees (UNHCR) was created.

We must find a way to manage this crisis in a more humane, equitable and organized manner. It is only possible if the international community is united and in agreement on how to move forward.

FILIPPO GRANDI
UNITED NATIONS
HIGH COMMISSIONER ON REFUGEES

UNHCR was established in 1950, initially as a temporary body to specifically and exclusively address the needs of forcibly displaced Europeans in the aftermath of World War II. Today UNHCR is a permanent body within the United Nations and its scope extends to all nations. There are various global players in the international refugee protection regime, but the primary organization is UNHCR.

In the 1970s the United States settled hundreds of thousands of Southeast Asian refugees through an ad hoc Refugee Task Force with temporary funding. The sheer volume of refugees prompted Congress to pass the Refugee Act of 1980,[1] the first comprehensive plan for refugee resettlement, which standardized resettlement services and created the US Refugee Admissions Program.

---

1. National Archives Foundation "Refugee Act of 1980," https://www.archivesfoundation.org/documents/refugee-act-1980/.

DEFINING "REFUGEES": THE 1951 REFUGEE CONVENTION

To begin our discussion on refugees it is important to know what we mean by "refugee." A refugee is someone seeking *asylum*, protection or shelter from danger. The inherent right of every human being to find protection when he needs it is at the heart of the international asylum and refugee protection regime. In 1951 the Refugee Convention, a multi-lateral treaty signed at a special United Nations conference in Geneva, Switzerland, put forth this international standard for defining refugee status and rights:[2]

> **Refugee:** someone who is unable or unwilling to return to his/her country of origin owing to a well-founded fear of being persecuted for reasons of race, religion, nationality, membership of a particular social group, or political opinion. A refugee is outside of his country of origin.

While the definition of terms like "fear" and "persecuted" were intentionally left vague to afford maximum protection to those who qualified, the scope of "refugee" was originally very narrow, applying only to Europeans displaced by WWII and to "events occurring before 1 January 1951." A 1967 Protocol removed the geographic and temporal limitation of the original 1951 Convention to make refugee protection more expansive. Refugee protection now applies to all nations.[3]

But refugees are only one type of forced migrant. Understanding the distinction between refugees and other types of migrants will help clarify the issues surrounding forced migration. Keep these definitions in mind whenever you listen to

RESETTLEMENT: the selection and transfer of refugees from a State in which they have sought protection to a third state which has agreed to them—as refugees—with permanent resident status.*

---

*   UNHCR Resettlement Handbook (2011), 3, www.unhcr.org/46f7c0ee2.pdf.

2. The United Nations Convention and Protocol provides this full definition of refugee in Article 1.A.2: For purposes of the present Convention, the term 'refugee' shall apply to a person who: (2) . . . owing to well founded fear of being persecuted for reasons of race, religion, nationality, membership in a particular social group or political opinion, is outside the country of his nationality and is unable or owing to such a fear, is unwilling to avail himself of the protection of that country; who, not having a nationality and being outside the country of his former habitual residence, is unable or, owing to such fear, is unwilling to return.

3. Refugee advocates disagree on what constitutes a "refugee." Some refugee advocates suggest the Refugee Convention needs to be broadened further still to include victims of environmental devastation, economic deprivation, or violence. This would result in an even greater number of those classified as "refugees."

conversations or news reports about "refugees." Generic application of the term can lead to misunderstanding about the population this workbook is addressing, that is, refugees that have been classified and vetted by the UNHCR and US governmental agencies. The following are different classifications of refugees:

> An *asylum seeker* has already entered the land where he seeks protection and is appealing for authorization to remain there. Asylum seekers have to be able to present a legitimate case for protection based on persecution, or they risk deportation.

> An *asylee* is a person who has legally received asylum. Asylees are eligible for Refugee Cash Assistance (RCA) and other benefits, like job training.

> An *internally displaced person* (IDP) has been forcibly removed from his home but remains within the boundaries of his country of origin. IDPs constitute the largest category of forced migrants, but there is no international legal instrument to protect them.

Debate revolves around the classification and evaluation of refugee status for those displaced by environmental factors. Some have conflated all causes for displacement and apply the term "refugee" generically to anyone who has been forced from their home. For instance, the category "environmental" or "climate" refugee has been introduced in more recent years as the plight of victims of environmental disasters has been brought to light. One source estimates that since 2008 an average of 26.4 million people have been displaced from their homes due to environmental disaster.[4] But the technical UNHCR definition for refugee applies only to those fleeing religious, political, and/or ethnic persecution. Currently there is no protocol for dealing with so-called "environmental refugees," even though their predicament is often tied with political factors. In 2016 the United States gave a first-ever grant to move a community impacted by climate change.[5]

Other persons of concern to the UNHCR are *stateless persons*—those who are not considered citizens of any political state under national laws, have no legal status, and are therefore deprived of many rights and benefits—and *returned refugees* (returnees) or *returned IDPs*—those who have returned voluntarily to their country of origin or area of habitual residence. Going home does not mean the need for protection has ended.

---

4. Internal Displacement Monitoring Center, http://www.internal-displacement.org/.

5. Carol Davenport and Campbell Robertson, "Resettling the First 'Climate Refugees,'" *New York Times*, May 3, 2016. http://www.nytimes.com/2016/05/03/us/resettling-the-first-american-climate-refugees.html (accessed October 22, 2016).

ASSESSING THE PROBLEM

What were the first words or images of refugees that you wrote down at the beginning of this chapter? Perhaps images of glassy-eyed masses stumbling out of boats. Perhaps bedraggled mobs limping across dusty desert. Perhaps terrorists come to mind.

One barrier to welcoming refugees is our perception of them. Our mental images are heavily influenced by the media, and while there are plenty of stories of the positive contributions of refugees, much that is out there is negative. Some of the negative stereotypes include portraying refugees as being:

- Culturally out-of-place—their religion, customs, and dress are unfamiliar, strange, even threatening.
- Economically burdensome—they benefit from public welfare and strain the system, resulting in less assistance for low-income American citizens.
- Politically threatening—we perceive them as a national security threat, especially as so many refugees today are from Muslim countries like Syria and Iraq, countries that have their own problem with extremism.
- Relationally taxing—refugees usually suffer from a range of symptoms resulting from PTSD (Post-Traumatic Stress Disorder). Many come over quite helpless and need to rely on others to help them assimilate.

It is hard to welcome someone if we have a perception that they are one or all of these things. Initially, worldwide population movements were viewed as a way to meet labor demands of growing economies. Today, however, a sudden influx of migrants to neighboring states is often viewed as a threat to national security, the economy, and cultural identity.

Refugees and national security was a major talking point in the 2016 presidential election. Republican party nominee Donald Trump proposed closing America's doors to outsiders, part of a plan to "Make America Great Again." Besides threatening to halt refugee admissions, especially from Syria, Trump proposed a temporary block of all Muslim immigration, mass deportation of undocumented immigrants, and a wall to keep out Mexicans. In an April 2016 speech in Rhode Island, Donald Trump mentioned that

---

The majority of those impacted by the climate crisis and move belong to the Biloxi-Chitimacha-Choctaw tribe, of Louisiana.

the state was resettling refugees, eliciting a chorus of boos. He then warned his audience, saying,

> We don't know where they're from . . . they have no documentation. We all have hearts and we can build safe zones in Syria and we'll get the Gulf States to put up the money . . . I'll get that done . . . We can't let this happen . . . Lock your doors . . . We don't know anything about 'em! . . . We have our incompetent government people letting 'em in by the thousands, and who knows, who knows, maybe it's ISIS.[6]

Meanwhile, several Democrats in the House of Representatives defied President Barack Obama's decision to raise the resettlement ceiling by voting for a bill that would halt Syrian refugee resettlement by adding an additional layer of screening to their vetting process. (The bill was later blocked by the Senate.) At least two Democratic governors opposed Syrian refugee resettlement in their states.

No matter your political persuasion, the reality is that refugees have come to America, and until the wars stop, refugees will continue to flow (not flood) into our country. In the past, refugee flows were thought to be temporary; today there are several protracted (long-lasting) situations all over the world, with refugees living in camps for five, ten, or over twenty-five years! The global community is facing a global quandary: as the number of forcibly displaced people increase, will the resources to care for them be available? Who is responsible for refugees? What is the best way to help them? We need to think seriously about our stance toward refugees.

Followers of Jesus have to consider not only political solutions but, more importantly, what the Bible teaches about caring for those who suffer. We need a theological perspective on the refugee crisis. Let's learn a little more about the history and current dynamics of the modern day refugee crisis, and then we'll look at what the Bible has to say about caring for refugees.

All human beings are born free and equal in dignity and rights. Everyone has the right to recognition everywhere as a person before the law. We recall that our obligations under international law prohibit discrimination of any kind on the basis of race, color, sex, language, religion, political or other opinion, national or social origin, property, birth or other status. Yet in many parts of the world we are witnessing, with great concern, increasingly xenophobic and racist responses to refugees and migrants.

New York Declaration I.13, UN Summit for Refugees and Migrants (2016)

---

6. Pamela Engel, "Trump on Syrian refugees: 'Lock your doors, folks,'" *Business Insider*, April 25, 2016. http://www.businessinsider.com/trump-syrian-refugees-isis-2016–4 (accessed October 26, 2016).

Personal Reflection:

1. Think of some areas in which globalization has impacted your daily life, both positively and negatively:

2. How does the United Nations define a refugee? What distinguishes a refugee from other types of forced migrants?

3. Write down one Scripture that speaks to how God might view refugees. If needed, use your concordance to look up key words "stranger," "sojourner," and/or "alien."

4. Pause for a moment and ask God to prepare your mind and heart to be challenged by this study. What does He want you to learn and how does He want you to respond? Ask him to remove any prejudices you may harbor.

CHAPTER 2
THE RUBBLED PLACES

The ruins in their hearts
Rehearse the rubbled places;
Our disordered times are
Recited by their faces.
The evils of our era
Are scrawled upon their features.
Who can scrub our History
From these ravaged creatures?
LOUIS GINSBERG **(1960)**

BEFORE WE BEGIN

Chapter 2 shares refugee stories and gives a picture of the scope of the global crisis. We'll also look back at historical mass migration movements.

Go to your computer and type two words into your browser: "refugee" and the name of your city. What do you find? Are there refugee agencies in your city? Do you find any articles about refugees in your city? If your city has refugees, what parts of the city do they live in? How large is the refugee community in your city? What countries to they come from? Do some research to answer these questions.

Sara, an engineering professor, grew up in conflict-ridden Iraq with seven siblings, all high academic achievers. Violence surged during the Iraq War of the 2000s, and when Sara started receiving death threats, she knew it was time to leave. She left Iraq for Egypt, returning home three months later to officially resign her university post. The day she decided to resign, her brother, also a professor, went missing. Tragically, he was later found dead.[7]

Santino is one of tens of thousands of "Lost Boys" who were orphaned during Sudan's civil war of the 1980s. Some of the Lost Boys walked miles on foot seeking refuge in neighboring Ethiopia and Kenya, many dying on the treacherous trek across the desert. Some of them were abducted or conscripted by both rebel and government armies and trained as child soldiers. In total 20,000 Lost Boys were displaced during the war.[8]

Victoria's mom was pregnant with her when she fled the civil war in Bosnia to the UK. Victoria's dad was held in a Serbian prison camp but later released. Between 1992–1995, over 200,000 Bosnians died in the horrific ethnic cleansing campaign.[9]

As these testimonies reveal, refugees come in all colors, ages, languages, and from all walks of life. And they each share a story of individual and collective suffering from circumstances they did not expect or deserve. These stories remind us that behind each individual human face is a personal story.

It would be a mistake to view refugees as a monolithic horde of faceless people. The word "refugee" is not a label we should use to completely define someone. Before fleeing, many refugees were doctors, engineers, artists, community activists, athletes. Refugees have dreams they still want to pursue, and they have the right to self-determination as much as any other person. Followers of Jesus believe that, ultimately, refugees are people made in the image of God.

Refugees are more than a statistic, but the numbers help us get a sense of the scope of the issue. This chapter provides numbers and facts on the current refugee crisis. As you read through the data, remember that behind each statistic is a human being made in the image of God, a human being whose story is worth telling.

> Refugee camps are like cities unto themselves, with their own economic, health, and education systems. Kenya hosts the world's largest camps, the Dadaab complex and Kakuma, which together house half a million refugees. The Kenyan government plans on closing Dadaab, potentially forcing refugees to return to areas of conflict.
>
> "LIFE IN LIMBO: INSIDE THE WORLD'S 10 LARGEST REFUGEE CAMPS," UNHCR. HTTP://STORYMAPS.ESRI .COM/STORIES/2016/REFUGEE-CAMPS/ (ACCESSED DECEMBER 8, 2016).

---

7. Personal interview with author. Name changed for privacy.

8. Megan Mylan and Jon Shenk, "Lost Boys of Sudan," (2004), 87 min. http://www.lostboysfilm.com/.

9. Beverly Naidoo, *Making It Home: Real-Life Stories from Children Forced to Flee* (New York: Dial Books, 2004), 19.

There are an estimated 65+ million forcibly displaced people worldwide:

- One-third of all displaced persons are classified as refugees.
- More than half of new refugees in 2015 were Syrians.
- Besides Syria, the majority of refugees come from Afghanistan, Iraq, Somalia, Democratic Republic of the Congo, and Myanmar.
- The majority of displaced persons are women and children.
- Millions of refugees have lived in protracted situations for decades.
- A majority of the world's refugees live in urban areas. About one quarter live in camps.[10]
- In fiscal year 2016 the United States admitted 84,995 refugees, with 70 percent originating from the Democratic Republic of the Congo, Syria, Myanmar (Burma), Iraq, and Somalia.[11]
- The majority of those granted asylum by the US come from China and Egypt.

SOURCES Global Trends: Forced Displacement in 2015 (UNHCR); Fact Sheet: Fiscal Year 2016 Refugee Admissions (state.gov)

GLOBAL FORCED DISPLACEMENT

The pie graph below illustrates the global percentages of the different categories of forced migrants. At the end of 2015, there were 65.3 million displaced people. Of them, 40.8 million were internally displaced persons (IDPs), constituting 62 percent of the world's displaced population. Refugees numbered 16.1 million (25 percent) and asylum seekers 3.2 million (5 percent). The remaining 5.2 million (8 percent) are refugees under the United Nations Relief and Works Agency for Palestine Refugees in the Near East (UNRWA), which addresses the needs of Palestinians uprooted after the establishment of the State of Israel (1948). The Palestinians, the world's oldest protracted refugee population (and at one time the largest, surpassed only recently by Syria), are under a special mandate separate from UNHCR.[12]

UNHCR defines a protracted refugee situation as one in which 25,000 or more refugees from the same nationality have been in exile for five or more years in a given asylum country.

---

10. UrbanRefugees.org, www.urban-refugees.org. Fifty-eight percent live in urban areas; twenty-eight percent in camps (accessed December 12, 2016).

11. The US fiscal year is October 1 to September 30.

12. United Nations Relief and Works Agency for Palestine Refugees in the Near East, established 1949, www.unrwa.org.

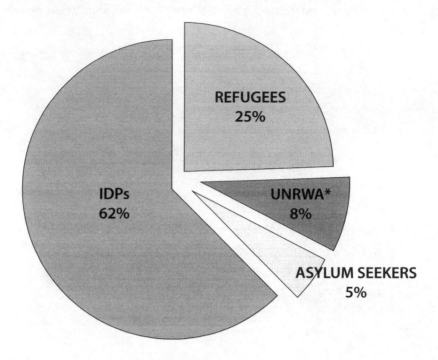

Source UNHCR Global Trends Report 2015
*Although most Palestinians under UNRWA are refugees by the technical definition of "refugee," they are placed in their own category because their mandate is separate from UNHCR.

Graph 1. Global Forced Displacement

> *Why is it helpful to know the distinction between the different types of forced migrants? In your opinion, which type of forced migrant makes the most compelling case for protection?*

HISTORICAL FORCED MIGRATION MOVEMENTS

The modern refugee movement originated in Europe, but over the past forty years, changes in global politics have created refugee movements in developing nations in Latin America, Africa, and Asia. This chart will familiarize you with some of the major historical refugee movements in the past century, and help you see why an international protocol was inevitable and necessary.

Table 1. Historical Forced Migration Movements[13]

1920s	• 1.5 M people flee the Russian Revolution • Armenians flee Turkish Asia Minor during Armenian genocide (first large-scale humanitarian effort in the US)
1930s	• Europeans flee totalitarian governments • Rise of Nazis
1940s	• WWII Nazi takeover of Europe. Holocaust. Results in over 40 M refugees • Exodus of Palestinians from homelands during Arab-Israeli conflict • 1947 Partition of India results in 14 M Muslims, Hindus, and Sikhs from Bangladesh, India, and Pakistan criss-crossing borders • 1949 Communist takeover in China
1950s	• Cold War • The Hungarian Revolution of 1956 prompts the first large-scale influx of refugees into the United States • Large number of African refugees in post-colonial era, continuing into the 1970s • Civil wars in Ethiopia, Somalia, the Great Lakes area of Africa • IDPs in Darfur, Sudan, due to civil war
1960s	• Civil wars in Angola, Rhodesia, Rwanda • Cuban Communist dictatorship • Latin American dictatorships
1970s	• Millions of "boat people" flee the Communist uprisings in Indochina • "Killing fields" of Cambodia 1975–79 • Bangladesh war of independence • Soviet invasion of Afghanistan
1980s	• Iran-Iraq War (1980–1988) • El Salvador, Guatemala, Haiti, Mexico: corruption, violence • Colombia, nation with one of the world's largest continuous populations of IDPs at 6M people*

---

13. Gil Loescher, *Beyond Charity*, Chapter 4; Lydia De Pillis, Kulwant Saluja, and Denise Lu "A Visual Guide to 75 years of major refugee crises around the world," *Washington Post*, https://www.washingtonpost.com/graphics/world/historical-migrant-crisis/ (accessed October 16, 2016); See also this infographic on the website for the US Committee for Refugees and Immigrants: http://refugees.org/explore-the-issues/refugees-facts/. Another good, concise source is UNHCR's webpage. Go to the tab "About UNHCR," then click "Facts and Figures about Refugees."

1990s	• Gulf War displaces 4.7 M Iraqis • Civil war in Mozambique • Breakup of Yugoslavia • Civil strife in Bangladesh, Tibet, Myanmar (Burma) • Rwandan genocide
2000s	• Bombing of World Trade Center and subsequent intervention in Afghanistan • Tsunami in Indonesia • Many of the refugee flows in the 2000s are ongoing from previous decades
2010s	• South Sudanese civil war • Ethnic and religious conflict in Central African Republic • Syrian uprising leaves 400,000 dead, 12 M displaced in 4 years • "Refugee highway": flows from Middle East to Europe and North America

*www.internal-displacement.org (accessed October 27, 2016). Syria only recently surpassed Colombia in numbers of total displaced IDPs.

As we have seen, a number of factors cause the number of refugees and the countries of origin of refugees to change over time. Less than a decade ago the composition of the world's refugees was quite different. In recent years, Afghanistan was producing the highest number of refugees. Today the greatest outflow of refugees is coming out of Syria, previously a relatively stable country. Syrians themselves never would have predicted this ten, even five years ago. Circumstances can change suddenly and unexpectedly.

> *Put yourself in the shoes of a refugee for a moment. Imagine what life would have been like as you fled your home country. What kind of assistance would you need? How would you want to be treated?*

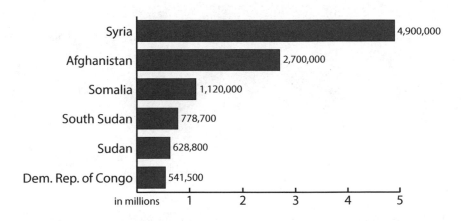

Source UNHCR Global Trends Report 2015.

Graph 2: Where do Refugees Come From?

ASSESSING THE REFUGEE CRISIS AT HOME

After a refugee is approved by UNHCR for resettlement in the US, individual states, non-governmental organizations (NGOs), and eleven voluntary agencies (VOLAGs) receive funding to provide resettlement services for refugees (see Appendix A for full list of VOLAGs). Many of these VOLAGs are faith-based, such as Catholic Charities, Episcopal Migration Ministries, and World Relief. In addition, churches, non-profits, and individuals contribute to refugee resettlement. The VOLAGs help mobilize concerned citizens to help refugees assimilate to their new lives.

One of the goals of this workbook is to provide a theological framework for caring for refugees that are resettled in America. In the next lesson, we'll look at what the Bible has to say about strangers. You'll discover that as followers of Jesus we have a lot more in common with refugees than we realize.

LEGAL RIGHTS OF REFUGEES
Article 31 of the 1951 Refugee Convention stipulates that refugees should not be penalized for illegal entry or stay, provided they can show just cause for their illegal entry or stay, because it recognizes that refugees may be forced to breach immigration rules in order to reach safety. Refugees are also protected under the principle of *non-refoulement*, meaning states have an obligation to not return refugees to nations from where they fled if there is fear of persecution or threat to life. The principle of not returning refugees is considered binding on all states, whether signatories to the Geneva Refugee Convention or not.*

---

*   Office of the United Nations High Commissioner for Refugees, The State of the World's Refugees: Human Displacement in the New Millenium, (Oxford: Oxford University Press, 2006), 33.

Personal Reflection

1. What new or unexpected information did you learn in this chapter?

2. Do you have personal contact with refugees? If so, how has knowing them impacted you?

3. Graph 2 shows the countries of origin for refugees today. Go back and look over the data, saying a short prayer for each country as you go down the list. Do some research on each country to learn the causes of the refugee crisis there. Table 1 will get you started.

CHAPTER 3
YOU ONCE WERE STRANGERS

For we are strangers before you
and sojourners, as all our fathers were.
Our days on the earth are like a shadow,
and there is no abiding.
1 CHRONICLES 29:15

BEFORE WE BEGIN

Is it possible that you have a lot in common with refugees? Chapter 3 will challenge you to think theologically about how God looks at the "stranger."

Give one biblical example of a refugee or sojourner. What were some of the challenges this person faced?

If you have ever travelled outside of your home country, what was it like being a "stranger" in a foreign land? Name both positive and negative experiences and impressions.

Jesus said the two Greatest Commandments were to love God with all your heart, soul, and mind, and to love your neighbor as yourself (Matt 22:36–40). As the Greatest Commandment, "Love God" is naturally the most oft-repeated commandment in the Hebrew Scriptures. "Welcome the stranger" is the second.[14] Does that come as a surprise to you?

Welcoming the stranger is a non-negotiable part of the Christian ethic. It's what Christians do, at least, it's what we're supposed to do. The Scriptures can help us reclaim that old religious vision of welcoming the stranger.[15]

We begin with the historical narrative of the Jewish people, whose story began with sojourning. You will recall that each of the great patriarchs spent part of his life as a stranger in a foreign land. God called Abram out of Ur of the Chaldeans to leave his country, relatives, and inheritance and go to Canaan (Gen 12). His long journey took him from Haran to Canaan, then to Egypt to escape a famine, then back toward Canaan, where he eventually settled and had Isaac (Gen 21). Isaac and his son Jacob lived as sojourners throughout Canaan for two generations until Jacob and his sons (the tribes of Israel) settled in Egypt, where they stayed for 400 years on account of a great famine (Gen 47). In Egypt they grew into a great nation. God eventually delivered Israel from Egyptian oppression through Moses, who led them toward the Promise Land. Along the journey, the Israelites encountered non-Israelites, some of whom chose to live among them as strangers.

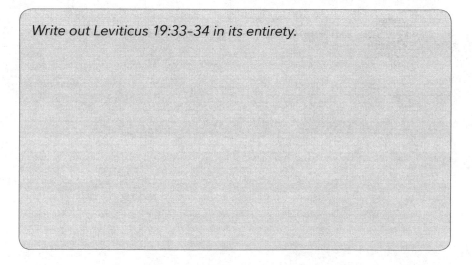

Write out Leviticus 19:33–34 in its entirety.

14. Matthew Soerens and Jenny Hwang, *Welcoming the Stranger: Justice, Compassion and Truth in the Immigration Debate* (Downers Grove: Intervarsity Press, 2009), 82.

15. This vision is shared by the three Abrahamic faiths. See the Qur'an 93:6–11 and Jonathan Sacks, "Mishpatim (5768)—Loving the Stranger," February 8, 2008, http://www.rabbisacks.org/covenant-conversation-5768-mishpatim-loving-the -stranger/ (accessed October 23, 2016).

"THE STRANGER WHO SOJOURNS AMONG YOU"

The Hebrew word for "stranger" is *ger*. Different Bible translations may also render the word *ger* as "alien," "foreigner," "guest," or "sojourner." In English, the most accurate translation of *ger* is "resident alien."[16] In the Israelite community, a *ger* was a person living outside of his home country who dwelled among the Israelites. The term generally referred to non-Israelites sojourning with the Israelites, but was also applied to the Israelites themselves when they sojourned in Egypt (Ex 2:22). The sojourner had abandoned his homeland for political or economic reasons and sought refuge among another community, as did Abraham in Hebron (Gen 23), Moses in Midian (Ex 22), Elimelech and his family in Moab (Ruth 1), and the Israelites in Egypt (Ex 1).

Ger is applied to those who settled in the land and sought the benefits and blessings of the land as prescribed by the Law of Moses. The sojourner travelling with the Israelites was expected to respect their laws and was entitled to their protection and provision. And just as he was to share in Israel's rejoicing (Deut 26:11), a *ger* was also subject to the laws of the land:

> For the assembly, there shall be one statute for you and for the stranger who sojourns with you, a statute forever throughout your generations. You and the sojourner shall be alike before the LORD. One law and one rule shall be for you and for the stranger who sojourns with you. (Num 15:15–16)[17]

Sojourners could participate in Jewish rituals as long as they followed Israel's laws for purification, circumcision, worship, and sacrifice (Deut 16:11, Ex 12:48). The Fourth Commandment makes provisions for strangers to enjoy Sabbath rest along with the Israelites so they may be refreshed (Ex 20:8, cf. Deut 5:14; Ex 23:12; Lev 16:29).

Israel played host to these foreign guests and was expected to protect, serve, love, and show hospitality to them. "You shall treat the stranger who sojourns with you as the native among you, and you shall *love him as yourself*, for you were strangers in the

Besides the commandment to love God, "welcome the stranger" was the second most oft-repeated command in the Hebrew Scriptures.

---

16. William D. Mounce, ed., *Mounce's Complete Expository Dictionary of Old & New Testament Words* (Grand Rapids: Zondervan, 2006).

17. Cf. Ex 12:49; Lev 24:22; Num 15:29.

land of Egypt: I am the LORD your God" (Lev 19:34, emphasis added). They were to provide for the stranger by dividing food, tithe, blessing, and land (Deut 26:12, Ezek 47: 21–23). The stranger did not have to earn his status to be treated with concern and respect—God commanded it (Lev 19:33–34).

You shall not pervert the justice due to the sojourner or to the fatherless...

DEUT 24:17

In legal matters, the Israelites were not to show partiality or withhold justice (Deut 1:17; 24:14,17; 27:19). The Bible very clearly mandated against mistreatment and oppression of strangers; in fact, some of Israel's blessings and judgment were contingent upon how they treated the stranger.[18] It was the Israelites' responsibility to make sure the poor and the stranger were provided for:

> When you reap the harvest of your land, you shall not reap your field right up to its edge, neither shall you gather the gleanings after your harvest. And you shall not strip your vineyard bare, neither shall you gather the fallen grapes of your vineyard. You shall leave them for the poor and for the sojourner: I am the LORD your God. (Lev 19:9–10; cf. Lev 23:22)[19]

Strangers among the Israelites were to be treated with equality, like natives of the land. So caring for refugees isn't just a compassion or pity issue—it's a justice issue. God in his righteous justice cares for all people, and so should we.

What is the basis for viewing caring for refugees as a justice issue? Do you agree with this assessment?

---

18. See Deut 24:19; 26:15; Jer 7:6; 22:3; Ezek 22:7,29; Zech 7:10; Mal 3:5.
19. Other provisions for the stranger: Deut 14:29; Deut 24:14–22.

LOVE JUSTICE, LOVE REFUGEES

Laws were set in place to protect sojourners among the Israelites. God's heart for justice was revealed through those laws and in the pronouncements he made against false justice (Isa 58). It's not enough to love the Word, study theology, tithe, share your faith, and abide by the law. It's not enough to do many things well—like the Pharisees—and yet lack one thing: "Woe to you . . . you hypocrites! You have a tenth of your spices— mint, dill and cumin. But you have neglected the more important matters of the law—justice, mercy and faithfulness" (Matt 23:23).

Jesus calls us beyond the letter of the law. Besides teaching the Greatest Commandment: "Love the Lord your God . . . Love your neighbor as yourself'" (Matt 22:37–39), Jesus also taught: "Love your enemies and pray for those who persecute you" (Matt 5:44). In the Parable of the Good Samaritan (Luke 10:25–37), a victim of violence was cared for and provided for by a Samaritan, considered to be an outsider to Jewish society. Jesus praised the Samaritan for being a true neighbor to the fallen man. In the same way, we fulfill the Greatest Commandment by caring and providing for those who have suffered much, especially those who are different from us.

During Jesus' earthly ministry he redefined social norms and overturned economic principles. He welcomed the outcast into his fellowship. He called people to give up their earthly treasures for a heavenly promise. He taught that the first would be last and the last would be first. He fed thousands with scraps of food. It is this kind of radical love and behavior that Jesus calls his followers into.

He has told you, O man, what is good; and what does the Lord require of you but to do justice, and to love kindness, and to walk humbly with your God?

MICAH 6:8

NO PROMISED LAND

From the first patriarch, Abraham, to Jesus and his disciples, and then to the Church, God has revealed himself as a God whose heart loves all the nations (Ps 2:8; Isa 51; John 3:16). In Genesis 12:1–3 God gives Abraham a calling:

> Now the LORD said to Abram, "Go from your country and your kindred and your Father's house to the land that I will show you. And I will make of you a great nation, and I will bless you and make your name great, so that you

will be a blessing. I will bless those who bless you, and him who dishonors you I will curse, and in you all the families of the earth shall be blessed."

God chose to bless Abraham by first turning him into a refugee. This was not a punishment but rather part of God's plan for the salvation of the nations (Acts 7:6). During his sojourn Abraham was compelled to seek the protection and favor of the Egyptians, Philistines, and Hittites. It appears to have been difficult at times for Abraham to see how God would fulfill his promise (Gen 16:2), but Abraham believed God and it was counted to him as righteousness (Rom 4:9).

In Genesis 12, when God called Abraham and his family out of his homeland, God made a promise to Abraham—that he would give him a land to possess and fill with his descendants, who would be as numerous as the stars in the sky. Abraham and his descendants spent most of their lives sojourning through what is now the Middle East before they were able to enter the Promised Land. Today, the Middle East is still the land of sojourn for millions of people, not because of promise, but as a consequence of war, conflict, and persecution.

Shortly after Jesus' birth King Herod issued an order to kill all infant boys in his attempt to get rid of the newborn king (Matt 2:13–14). Jesus, Mary, and Joseph fled from Galilee and found refuge in Egypt. And Jesus wasn't a refugee just once. In fact, his entire existence on earth was a sojourning experience. Jesus said, "Foxes have holes, and birds of the air have nests, but the Son of Man has nowhere to lay his head" (Matt 8:20). During his ministry years, Jesus was constantly on the move from those who would do him harm. Our Lord and Savior himself lived the experience of a refugee!

"YOU WERE ONCE STRANGERS"

As you can see, the sojourner metaphor is deeply embedded within the history and theology of the Jewish people. Being a stranger and sojourner is part of her national identity, and so to us followers of Jesus Christ it gets transmitted down to us as heritage:

- "You shall not oppress a sojourner. You know the heart of a sojourner, for you were sojourners in the land of Egypt" (Ex 23:9).
- "For you are strangers and sojourners with me" (Lev 25:23).

- "For I am a sojourner with you, a guest, like all my fathers" (Ps 39:12).
- "I am a sojourner on the earth" (Ps 119:19).
- "Beloved, I urge you as sojourners and exiles to abstain from the passions of the flesh, which wage war against your soul" (1 Pet 2:11).

The stranger motif is powerful because it describes our relationship to God before Christ, as well as our relationship to our heavenly home. Before Christ, Gentiles (the nations) "were separate from Christ, excluded from citizenship in Israel and foreigners to the covenants of the promise, without hope and without God in the world" (Eph 2:12). But then God adopted us into His family through Jesus Christ and we are "no longer strangers and aliens" (Eph 2:19). Christ has torn down the separating wall and we are no longer strangers to God (Eph 2:14). Resist, then, the urge to allow the word "refugee" to become a label that creates a wall between you and the stranger.

The heart of God toward strangers back then and today is that of a loving and protective Father. Strangers are under His divine protection (Ps 146:9). Christians today are called to have this same heart towards strangers: "[God] executes justice for the fatherless and the widow, and loves the sojourner, giving him food and clothing. Love the sojourner, therefore, for you were sojourners in the land of Egypt" (Deut 10:18–19). Throughout Scripture the Lord reminds his people that they, too, had once been in the same needy position as the stranger.

Like refugees, all we who are in Christ are considered sojourners, aliens, and pilgrims on earth (1 Chr 29:15; 1 Pet 1:17). Like the giants of the faith listed in Hebrews 11, we acknowledge that we are strangers and exiles. Yet as strangers and exiles we are not aimless, nor are we hopeless. Rather, we desire a better country, a heavenly one (Heb 11:16). As sojourners we make no claim to this life or this land. We recognize that everything we have is by God's will and by his grace. And so we fix our eyes on heaven, where our true citizenship lies: "Our citizenship is in heaven, and from it we await a Savior, the Lord Jesus Christ" (Phil 3:20).

We can relate with refugees because we, too, have no permanent home in this life. This is what we have in common—we are all looking for a better country. And by that token we all depend on the grace of God.

Personal Reflection

1. How does the biblical treatment of "strangers" impact the way you view refugees?

2. How does Jesus' own identification as a refugee and as a sojourner on earth impact the way you view refugees? How does it impact the way you view yourself?

3. Who are the "strangers" in your life? Who are people you encounter on a regular basis that perhaps you have been avoiding or have not extended a welcome to?

4. In what ways are you behaving too much like a citizen of the earth rather than a citizen of heaven in search of a better country? Are you holding on to certain rights, privileges, or material things that aren't rightly yours to claim? Pray and ask God to reveal this to you. Respond with humility knowing that God looks upon us with compassion.

CHAPTER 4
THE PILGRIM'S PROBLEM

If we knew the stories of refugees,
they would break our hearts.
GARRISON KEILLOR

BEFORE WE BEGIN

Chapter 4 looks at adversities faced by refugees. As you read this chapter try to imagine yourself in the shoes of refugees who have found themselves in these dire predicaments.

In the last lesson, we identified with refugees out of our own sojourner heritage as the people of God. What are some common challenges faced by sojourners on the move?

Imagine leaving your homeland for a new country. What would you miss leaving behind the most?

On May 13, 1939, the *St. Louis* sailed from Germany to Cuba with 937 refugees on board. Almost all passengers were Jews fleeing the Third Reich. Most held landing certificates and transit visas issued by the Cuban government, unaware that a week prior the Cuban president had invalidated their legal documents. Denied entry by Cuba, the *St. Louis* headed toward Miami to seek refuge in the United States. The pleas to admission by an American Jewish refugee organization, the ship's captain, and the passengers were to no avail—the *St. Louis* was forced to sail back to Europe. The passengers were admitted to four Western European countries where they were interned in labor camps or forced to go into hiding. Some were later able to emigrate to North America or Australia. Many were later deported and exterminated in Nazi concentration camps after the German invasion of Western Europe.[20]

Three-quarters of a century later, on April 19, 2015, a small vessel set sail from Libya, steering toward Italy. The boat, dangerously overloaded with migrants and refugees, capsized, leading to the deaths of an estimated 800 people in the waters of the Mediterranean Sea, the deadliest disaster there to date.[21] One year later, during three consecutive days, three more boats capsized, plunging 700 migrants to their watery graves.[22] Between 2013 and 2016 at least 10,000 migrants lost their lives trying to cross the sea.[23]

Many questions arise from the tragic stories of the *St. Louis* and the Mediterranean Sea crossings: Did the refugees have a "right" to seek refuge abroad? Do the countries where they are trying to land have a moral obligation to admit them? How does a state struggling internally with low employment and recession handle immigration requests? How does a state counter xenophobia, racism, and fear? These and other questions reveal that there is no simple solution to the refugee crisis.

---

20. For more on the *St. Louis*, search the United States Holocaust Memorial Museum website: http://www.ushmm.org.

21. Alessandro Bonomolo and Stephanie Kirchgaessner, "U.N. says 800 migrants dead in boat disaster as Italy launches rescue of two more vessels," *The Guardian*, April 20, 2015, https://www.theguardian.com/world/2015/apr/20/italy-pm-matteo-renzi-migrant-shipwreck-crisis-srebrenica-massacre (accessed October 24, 2016).

22. Patrick Kingsley, "More than 700 migrants feared dead in Mediterranean sinkings," *The Guardian*, May 29, 2016, https://www.theguardian.com/world/2016/may/29/700-migrants-feared-dead-mediterranean-says-un-refugees (accessed October 24, 2016).

23. Missing Migrants Project, https://missingmigrants.iom.int/mediterranean (accessed October 26, 2016).

Did the passengers have a "right" to seek refuge abroad? What emotions get stirred as you read about these tragedies?

NO EASY SOLUTIONS

Ultimately the goal of UNHCR is to ensure refugees' access to protection and a *durable solution*. UNHCR seeks to employ one of three durable solutions:

- *Voluntary repatriation*, or assisting a refugee to return to his country of origin, is viewed as the most ideal durable solution to reducing displacement.
- *Local integration* means naturalization of the refugee into his country of asylum.
- *Resettlement* into a second or third host country is a protection tool for refugees who are unable or unwilling to return to their country of origin.

Refugees and asylum seekers encounter barriers to all three durable solutions. Even if a refugee were repatriated, it is back to a home that has been devastated by war, a place that is at once familiar and unfamiliar. And while it may seem from the news media that refugees are being easily resettled in hordes into the US, the truth is only about 1 percent of all refugees globally in any given year are resettled in a third country.

> A durable solution is one that will enable refugees to live in safely and rebuild their lives.*

Some refugees who really need protection have a difficult time seeking asylum because of the unpredictable and chaotic nature of forced migration. Many refugees are either ignorant of asylum laws, or are erroneously warned to go into hiding for fear of immediate deportation. Upon arrival, an asylum seeker has to prove to an asylum officer that he has "credible fear" of persecution, and is for that reason seeking refuge in the US. If no case for credible

---

* United Nations High Commissioner for Refugees, http://www.unhcr.org/en-us/solutions.html.

fear can be made, he is deported. If he is allowed to stay, he may be held like a prisoner in a detention center with convicted criminals for months or years until he can make a claim in front of a judge. The poor treatment and conditions in these jails often re-traumatize the asylum seeker.

Women and children are especially at risk. Women and children make up the majority of the world's refugees and IDPs. Half of global refugees are children, many of them unaccompanied or separated. Women and children are more susceptible to forms of gender-based violence and discrimination, such as human trafficking, theft, extreme poverty, sexual assault, and lack of education and health care.

MY BROTHER'S KEEPER?

The issue of burden sharing has been a long-standing issue in the refugee protection regime. Currently the United States is the top receiving country of refugees for resettlement. While the US contributes to alleviating the refugee crisis by being the top resettlement country, most of the hosting, or housing, burden is shouldered by developing countries, which host 86 percent of all refugees. In fact 26 percent of refugees are hosted in the world's *least* developed countries. For many years, Pakistan shouldered the largest burden of refugee hosting (mostly Afghan). In just the past year, Turkey surpassed Pakistan to become the country with the largest hosting burden, now with 2.5 million refugees, mostly Syrian. The next countries hosting the largest numbers of refugee are Lebanon, Iran, and Ethiopia.[24] In the past few years Europe has been inundated with asylum seekers fleeing the Middle East. Germany took in 1.1 million asylum seekers in just one year, 2015, sparking intense debate over how to manage the migrant crisis.[25]

In terms of which countries host the highest number of refugees per 1000 residents, small countries like Lebanon (#1), Jordan (#2), and Nauru (in Micronesia, #3) hold that distinction.[26] Nearly 20 percent of Lebanon's population is composed of refugees.[27] Meanwhile countries hosting

---

24. United Nations High Commissioner for Refugees, *2015 Global Trends*.

25. Patrick Donahue and Arne Delfs, "Germany Saw 1.1 Million Migrants in 2015 as Debate Intensifies," *Bloomberg*, January 6, 2016, https://www.bloomberg.com/news/articles/2016–01–06/germany-says-about-1–1-million-asylum-seekers-arrived-in-2015 (accessed December 12, 2016).

26. United Nations High Commissioner for Refugees. *2015 Global Trends*.

27. Ibid.

the most refugees per 1 USD GDP (PPP) per capita—countries like the Democratic Republic of the Congo (471), Ethiopia (453), and Pakistan (317)—are among the nations with the lowest ranked national GDPs.[28]

UNHCR considers it vital for industrialized states to shoulder a larger portion of the refugee problem, as safeguards to asylum are less stable in developing countries.[29] The United States has historically received the highest total number and percentage of refugees for resettlement of any country in the world. The chart below shows recent numbers for resettlement burden sharing. The countries listed are consistently among the highest receiving nations. Notice that totals for 2015 increased from the year prior for most of the top ten resettlement countries.

Table 2. UNHCR Resettlement Statistics by Resettlement Country
CY (Calendar Years) 2014 and 2015

Country	Totals for CY2014	Totals for CY2015	Percent of Total Resettled CY2015	Rank Per Capita 2015 Per 1000 pp
Totals	73,008	81,893	100.00%	
United States*	48,911	52,583	64.21%	5
Canada	7,233	10,236	12.50%	1
Australia	6,162	5,211	6.36%	4
Norway	3,167	2,220	2.71%	2
Germany	1,497	2,097	2.56%	17
Sweden	1,188	1,808	2.21%	6
United Kingdom	1,011	1,768	2.16%	15
Finland	743	964	1.18%	7
New Zealand	632	756	0.92%	8
Other	2,164	4,250	5.19%	

Source US Department of State, Proposed Refugee Admissions for Fiscal Year 2017; Refugee Council of Australia
*Figures may vary slightly from UNHCR numbers. Country figures may include submissions outside of UNHCR auspices or omit instances where UNCHR assisted, not submitted, a case.
**These figures reflect calendar year statistics. The US fiscal year is October 1 to September 30.

---

28. GDP (PPP) refers to Gross Domestic Product (Purchasing Power Parity). See Fig. 5 in *2015 Global Trends: Forced Displacement in 2015* (UNHCR: 2016).

29. Office of the United Nations High Commissioner for Refugees, *The State of the World's Refugees*, 61.

> *What are your concerns, if any, about refugee resettlement and national security?*

THE VETTING PROCESS

One of the major controversies surrounding the refugee debate has to do with national security concerns, that by welcoming refugees our government ends up facilitating avenues for terrorism to slip in as well. This could not be farther from the truth. In fact, refugees are the most strictly screened immigrant group to enter the US. Here is the truth regarding the vetting process for refugees:[30]

- It is an extensive and lengthy process.
- Refugees are security screened by several different agencies.
- Refugees are also health screened for contagious diseases.
- Refugees do not get to choose where they are resettled.
- Less than one percent of the global refugee population is ultimately approved for resettlement.

A refugee's first point of contact is with UNHCR, who determines where to resettle refugees based on presence of family members and other factors. Under the guidance of the US Department of State's Bureau of Population, Refugees, and Migrants, an in-country Resettlement Support Center (RSC) conducts initial interviews with the refugees. Those designated for the US are vetted by several governmental entities: the Departments of State, Homeland Security, and Defense; the National Counterterrorism Center; and the FBI's Terrorist Screening Center. (As of 2016 Syrians were undergoing additional security screenings.) After approval by the US Citizenship and Immigration Services (USCIS) and passing a health screening, refugees are almost ready for departure.

---

30. See this helpful infographic, "Security Screening of Refugees Admitted to the United States": http://refugees.org/wp-content/uploads/2015/12/USCRI-Security-Screening-Process-5.16.16.pdf.

They must complete a cultural orientation, secure sponsorship assurances from a refugee agency in the US, and finally are referred to the International Organization for Migration (IOM) to make travel arrangements. Refugees sign a promissory note to repay their travel fees—on an interest-free loan—within 46 months after arrival in the US. The entire process takes on average 18–24 months.[31]

These facts should allay fears and clear up misconceptions surrounding the stringency of refugee admissions. As you can see, a terrorist trying to enter the US through a resettlement program has chosen a rather cumbersome pathway.

KNOWLEDGE LEADS TO ACTION

Refugees are too often seen as criminals, rather than victims of the worst circumstances. Our perceptions of refugees have long shaped our national policy towards admissions and resettlement. America, while being in many ways a welcoming nation, was not only slow to sign on to the UN refugee regime, at times it was hostile.[32] From the late 1950s to the 1980 Cuban boatlift, 800,000 Cubans fleeing Communism under Castro were given virtually automatic amnesty.[33] On the contrary, Haitians fleeing the "Papa Doc" Duvalier regime around the same time were considered politico-economic refugees, not political refugees, despite overwhelming evidence of human rights abuses in Haiti.[34] They were classified as "no status" and later deported, detained until they could be expelled, or intercepted at sea. The preferential treatment of the Cubans over the Haitians was also influenced by America's ideological stance against Communism.

The world will not be destroyed by those who do evil, but by those who watch them without doing anything.

ALBERT EINSTEIN

It is too easy to sympathize with the plight of refugees for a moment, only to soon forget about them. Geographical distance makes their struggle feel like "that" problem "over there." Bombardment by news

---

31. International Organization for Migration, https://www.iom.int/countries /united-states-america (accessed October, 22, 2016). The vast majority of refugees are able to pay back their loans within 46 months. While it might seem harsh to expect them to pay back their travel loans, the repayment is what helps the US continue to assist other refugees.

32. Loescher, *Beyond Charity*, 55 and 64.

33. Ibid., 100.

34. Animesh Ghoshal and Thomas M. Crowley, "Refugees and Immigrants: A Human Rights Dilemma," *Human Rights Quarterly*, Vol. 5, No. 3 (August 1983), 337.

media results in "compassion fatigue." Yet if we focus on their humanity and put ourselves in their shoes as fellow sojourners, it is easier to respond to the refugee crisis with compassion and generosity. Ordinary citizens can be a vessel of grace through small acts of kindness and hospitality. Former US Special Representative for Religion and Global Affairs Shaun Casey has stated:

> Despite the negative anti-refugee rhetoric that has been prevalent in US media and political discourse recently, many local refugee resettlement offices report that they continue to receive an outpouring of support from community members. It is innovative, 'whole of society' collaboration and support at the local level—from religious leaders and communities, non-governmental organizations, social service providers, schools, police departments, municipal government leaders, and individual volunteers—that continues to make the refugee resettlement process possible and successful.[35]

You've just absorbed a lot of information about the refugee crisis, but knowledge alone is not enough to make a difference. Difference requires action. The next chapter looks at the history of refugees in the United States. Chapter 6 and the Personal Action Plan will challenge you to get involved in your local context and beyond.

THE BOATMAN

We were thirty-one souls all, he said,
    on the gray-sick of sea
in a cold rubber boat, rising and falling in our filth.
By morning this didn't matter, no land was in sight,
all were soaked to the bone, living and dead.
We could still float, we said, from war to war.
What lay behind us but ruins of stone
    piled on ruins of stone?
City called "mother of the poor" surrounded by fields
of cotton and millet, city of jewelers and cloak-makers,
with the oldest church in Christendom
    and the Sword of Allah.

---

35. Personal email exchange with Office of Religion and Global Affairs, US Department of State

If anyone remains there now, he assures,
>   they would be utterly alone.
There is a hotel named for it in Rome
>   two hundred meters
from the Piazza di Spagna, where you
>   can have breakfast under
the portraits of film stars. There the staff
>   cannot do enough for you.
But I am talking nonsense again, as
>   I have since that night
we fetched a child, not ours, from the sea, drifting face-
down in a life vest, its eyes taken by
>   fish or the birds above us.
After that, Aleppo went up in smoke,
>   and Raqqa came under a rain
of leaflets warning everyone to go.
>   Leave, yes, but go where?
We lived through the Americans and
>   Russians, through Americans
again, many nights of death from the
>   clouds, mornings surprised
to be waking from the sleep of death,
>   still unburied and alive
but with no safe place. Leave, yes, we
>   obey the leaflets, but go where?
To the sea to be eaten, to the shores
>   of Europe to be caged?
To *camp misery* and *camp remain* here.
>   I ask you then, where?
You tell me you are a poet. If so, our
>   destination is the same.
I find myself now the boatman, driving
>   a taxi at the end of the world.
I will see that you arrive safely, my
>   friend, I will get you there.[36]

---

36. "The Boatman," by Carolyn Forché. First published in *Poetry*, October 2016. Used by permission.

Personal Reflection

1. Respond to the opening story about the St. Louis and the Mediterranean Sea crossings. What solutions would you propose in those situations?

2. The US is currently the top resettlement country. Geographically, culturally, and linguistically-speaking, the United States is one of the most distant countries from the source countries of refugees. Does the US—one of the world's most developed and wealthiest nations yet with our own poverty issues—have a moral obligation to admit refugees today?

3. In your honest opinion, are refugees a burden to society? Explain.

4. Where are you feeling challenged most as you go through this study? What perspective has shifted for you, either positively or negatively?

CHAPTER 5
ALL THE WORLD IS HERE

But, though the conflict prove severe,
Let pilgrims resolute be found;
For succor will, at length, appear,
And they with vict'ry shall be crown'd.
JOHN BUNYAN, The Pilgrim's Progress

BEFORE WE BEGIN

Chapter 5 reflects upon our nation's rich history of refugees. We look at how the nations have always come to the US, how they are coming even more so now, and what implications that has for us who follow Jesus.

Unless you belong to an indigenous people, you have an immigrant heritage. Write down how and when your family came to the US.

In what ways does your immigrant heritage impact your identity and self-understanding?

The Commonwealth of Massachusetts has a rich history of refugees, going back several centuries to America's original refugees, known to us as "Pilgrims."

The Pilgrims fled religious persecution in England and came to America to establish free communities of worship, landing at Plymouth Harbor, Massachusetts, in 1620.

In the early 1800s visionaries grew a booming textile industry in Lowell, later dubbed the "Cradle of the American Industrial Revolution." The area began welcoming European immigrants to grow the economy. However, the southward shift of the national textile industry in the 1920s and the Great Depression of the 1930s hit Lowell hard, and its economy flattened. The historic mill town of Lowell withered to just a shadow of its earlier glory days.

In the 1970s, the Khmer Rouge instigated a genocide in Cambodia, leading to the death and displacement of millions of Cambodians. A large number were resettled in Lowell. The high-tech boom of that decade and the decision of Wang Laboratories to build their world headquarters in Lowell created low-wage computer assembly jobs requiring low skills and no English. Refugees settled there were able to find jobs.

There was a significant secondary migration to Lowell as more Cambodians reconnected with long-lost family and friends. Since 1980, refugee resettlement and immigration have drastically impacted Lowell. In 1980 the ethnic minority population was less than 5 percent; thirty years later, non-whites represent 30 percent of the city. Between 1980 and 2000, the Asian population alone increased by an astonishing 2,876 percent![37] Most of Lowell's Asian population is Cambodian. In fact, Lowell boasts the second largest Cambodian population in America (the first is Long Beach, CA).[38]

Today, Lowell is one of the most ethnically diverse cities in the Commonwealth, with Asians constituting 21.4 percent of its population.[39] Through the assistance of nonprofit organizations like the International Institute of Lowell and the Cambodian Mutual Assistance Association, the Cambodian refugee population has been able to establish a thriving community in this New England town that not so long ago was flailing in recession.

---

37. Mary Yu Donico, ed., *Asian American Society: An Encyclopedia* (Thousand Oaks: SAGE Publications, Inc., 2014), "Cambodian Americans."

38. Cambodian Mutual Assistance Association, http://www.cmaalowell.org /aboutus.html (accessed October 20, 2016).

39. University of Massachusetts Boston Institute for Asian American Studies, "Population of Asian Americans in Selected Cities and Towns in Massachusetts," https://www.umb.edu/iaas/census/2010/population_of_asian_americans_cities _towns_in_ma (accessed October 20, 2016).

WHO'S COMING TO AMERICA?

In the aftermath of World War II the United States took in hundreds of thousands of Europeans who had been displaced by the war. In total, over 650,000 refugees were admitted following the enactment of the Displaced Persons Act of 1948. But America initially withheld from signing the 1951 Refugee Convention because it did not reflect our ideological stance against Communism. It was not until 1965 that the new Immigration and Nationality Act increased quotas of immigrants from non-European nations. Refugee admissions, however, were not greatly impacted by it. The 1980 Refugee Reform Act created the Office of Refugee Resettlement, and the US increased yearly caps and finally complied with the 1967 Protocol.

Refugee admissions are affected by several factors. World events, politics, racism, public sympathy, and political atmosphere all play into admission decisions. One of the determining factors for where refugees are placed has to do with native community. Refugees are often resettled en masse in a particular area of the country so they can maintain cultural ties and reunite with family and friends. Refugees are sometimes resettled in an area where they can continue in the industry of their country of origin. The resettlement of refugees to an area can have significant impact on its cultural, economic, and demographic identity.

Since 1975, the US has resettled over three million refugees.[40] In the past decade, the Burmese have been the largest group of refugees resettled to the United States with 148,957 (or 24 percent of total resettled) since 2006. The next two groups are Iraqis (125,970, or 20 percent) and Bhutanese (84,547, or 14 percent).[41]

While it's Muslim refugees that are dominating the news right now, many Americans do not even realize that many former and incoming refugees to America are Christian.[42] The Burmese and Bhutanese—

---

40. Refugee Processing Center data, www.wrapsnet.org. You can pull up a variety of reports on this website.

41. Jie Zong and Jeanne Batalova, "Refugees and Asylees in the United States," Migration Policy Institute, October 28, 2015, http://www.migrationpolicy.org /article/refugees-and-asylees-united-states#Admissions Process (accessed October 22, 2016).

42. Morgan Lee, "Here's Where America's 338,000 Christian Refugees Come From," *Christianity Today*, November 20, 2015, http://www.christianitytoday.com /gleanings/2015/november/heres-where-americas-338000-christian-refugees-have -come.html (accessed October 1, 2016).

and even some of the Iraqis—are largely Christian minority groups who had been persecuted in their home country. Refugees like them—and many others—are therefore our persecuted brothers and sister in Christ, and they come as a prophetic voice and blessing to the Church in America. Today independent immigrant churches are the fastest growing among evangelical churches in the US.[43] The Catholic Church in America, of which 25 percent were born outside of the country, is bolstered by, if not dependent upon, the presence of immigrants and refugees for their revitalization.[44] So Christian refugees are not just our guests, they are our brothers and sisters. They are changing the landscape, not just of our nation, but also of our churches.

> *We, the community of faith, are judged by the way we treat the most vulnerable among us . . . Our church communities must find pastoral and legal ways to welcome our brothers and sisters in faith.*
>
> STRANGERS NO LONGER
> CATHOLIC DOCUMENT ON MIGRATION

Refugee arrivals

Each year, the President of the United States, after consulting with Congress and sets admissions ceilings on how many refugees from which nationality will be accepted for resettlement. The table and graph below show refugee arrivals by nationality and year. In fiscal year 2016, the US resettled 84,995 refugees. The states that received the largest number of refugees were California (9.3%), Texas (9.2%), New York (5.9%), Arizona (5.0 %), Florida (4.9%) and Michigan (4.8%).[45] Graph 3 reveals the proposed admissions trends over the past 20 years. Note the changes in nationalities of arriving refugees between the years 2006 and 2016 (Table 3), as well as the dip in refugee admissions in the early 2000s following the 9/11 attacks (Graph 3). In the next few years, the US expects to see an increase in Syrian refugees.

---

43. Todd M. Johnson, "USA Evangelicals/Evangelicals in a Global Context," *Lausanne World Pulse* (January 2006).

44. Tom Gjelten and Marisa Peñaloza, "Built by Immigrants, US Catholic Churches Bolstered by Them Once Again," National Public Radio, September 9, 2015, http://www.npr.org/2015/09/09/437219447/built-by-immigrants-u-s-catholic-churches-bolstered-by-them-once-again (accessed October 23, 2016).

45. US Department of State, Refugee Processing Center. Retrieved from Interactive Reports, Refugee Arrivals for fiscal year 2016, http://ireports.wrapsnet.org (accessed April 6, 2017).

Table 3. Refugee Arrivals to the US by Country of Nationality
(Fiscal Years 2016 and 2006)

Country	2016 Number	Percent	2006 Number	Percent
Admissions ceiling	85,000		70,000	
Total arrivals	84,995	100%	41,223	100%
DR Congo	16,370	19.3	66	0.2
Syria	12,587	14.8	27	0.1
Myanmar (Burma)	12,347	14.5	1,612	3.9
Iraq	9,880	11.6	202	0.5
Somalia	9,020	10.6	10,357	25.1
Bhutan	5,817	6.8	—	—
Iran	3,750	4.4	2,792	6.8
Afghanistan	2,737	3.2	651	1.6
Ukraine	2,543	3.0	2,483	6.0
Eritrea	1,949	2.3	538	1.3
Other	7,995	9.4%	22,495	54.6%

Source US Department of State, Refugee Processing Center, fiscal year 2016.
Note In 2006, three of the largest source countries were Russia (6,003), Vietnam (3,168), and Cuba (3,143)

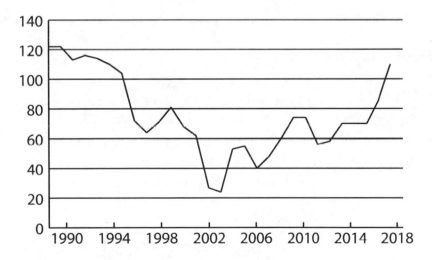

Source US Department of State, Refugee Processing Center, fiscal year 2016.

Graph 3. Refugee Admissions to the US
1990 to 2016 (in ten thousands)

How do you feel about the increasing numbers of Muslim refugees being resettled in the US?

The nations have come

9/11 AND REFUGEE ADMISSIONS:

Following the September 11, 2001, attacks on the World Trade Center in New York City, refugee admissions were temporarily halted as the nation reassessed its security plans regarding admitting foreigners. In 1990, the US admitted 122,000 refugees; in 2002 only 27,110 were admitted, a 25-year low. Since 2004, the numbers have steadily increased but are still lower than they were in the 1980s and 90s.

US DEPT OF STATE, BUREAU OF POPULATIONS, REFUGEES AND MIGRATION (PRM): 2009

International policy can facilitate the entry of refugees into our country, but once they are here, it is resettlement agencies and concerned citizens who make a difference in how well refugees assimilate. Nine different non-profit agencies, six of them faith-based, help refugees settle in the US (See Appendix A for a complete list.) The agencies help refugees find housing and jobs but they also highly depend on volunteers to assist with the resettlement process, from setting up apartments to teaching ESL.

The nations have come to America, creating a tremendous opportunity for us to live out our faith and commitment to Christ. The last words of Jesus before his Ascension were, "But you will receive power when the Holy Spirit has come upon you, and you will be my witnesses in Jerusalem and in all Judea and Samaria and to the end of the earth" (Acts 1:8). Today, the ends of the earth are coming to America, and you have the opportunity to show God's love to them, without leaving your home. What is your vision for making the most of that opportunity?

We distinguish that the refugees fleeing this violence are not our enemies; they are victims. We call for Christians to support ministries showing the love of Jesus to the most vulnerable, those in desperate need, and the hurting. This is what Jesus did; He came to the hurting and brought peace to those in despair.

Critical moments like these are opportunities for us to be like Jesus, showing and sharing His love to the hurting and the vulnerable in the midst of this global crisis. Thus we declare that we care, we are responding because our allegiance is to Jesus, and we seek to be more like Him, emulating His compassionate care for the most vulnerable.[46]

46. Ed Stetzer, "Christian Declaration on Caring for Refugees: An Evangelical Response," GC2 Summit Statement, http://www.christianitytoday.com/edstetzer /2016/january/church-leaders-speak-on-refugees.html.

Personal Reflection

1. With continuing immigration into the United States, how can Christians in America view this as an opportunity to live out their faith?

2. Would you advocate for more or fewer refugees being resettled in our country? In your city? Why or why not?

3. Why is making yourself knowledgeable about a refugee's background so crucial?

4. Stop and say a prayer for the persecuted global Church.

CHAPTER 6
SERVING ANGELS

*Faith in God's love toward man is perfected
in man's love to God and neighbor.*
H. Richard Niebuhr

BEFORE WE BEGIN

Our final chapter will look at the role of hospitality in the redemption narrative of Scripture, and how that applies to us today in regard to refugees.

Recall a time when you received another's generosity or hospitality. What type of impression did it leave on you?

Name at least one biblical basis for practicing hospitality:

Imagine you are at seated at a rich banquet table. The linen is freshly pressed and silky to the touch. Food overflows the silver platters and the air is sweet with the aroma of wine. A melodic tune plays overhead while graceful servers delicately spoon the meal onto your plate. The food is exquisite, the service impeccable. This is a meal you can never repay, for the host cannot be repaid. He is too great and too generous.

This is what it is like at the Lord's Table. At the Lord's Table the Lord is the host, and we are his guests. As host, the Lord is the one who opens his home and provides for his people. We live by God's invitation and in his company and in his favor—God is the divine host and Israel is his perpetual guest (Lev 25:23; Ps 15:1; 39:12; Matt 22:1–14).[47]

Most [evangelical Christians] see newcomers as a threat or a burden. Only 4 in 10 see a gospel opportunity.

MATTHEW SOERENS, WORLD RELIEF

As God's ambassadors, Christians reflect God's hospitality to the stranger when we function as host. Thus, exercising hospitality is exercising our faith. These verses point out the significance of hospitality to our Christian ethic:

- "Show hospitality to one another without grumbling" (1 Pet 4:9).
- "Contribute to the needs of the saints and seek to show hospitality" (Rom 12:13).
- "Do not neglect to show hospitality to strangers . . . Do not neglect to do good and to share what you have, for such sacrifices are pleasing to God" (Heb 13:2,16).
- "Bear one another's burdens, and so fulfill the law of Christ" (Gal 6:1).
- "So then, as we have opportunity, let us do good to everyone, and especially to those who are of the household of faith" (Gal 6:10).
- "Beloved, it is a faithful thing you do in all your efforts for these brothers, strangers as they are . . ." (3 John 5).

THE ROLE OF HOSPITALITY IN THE REDEMPTION NARRATIVE

In Genesis chapter 18, Abraham is sitting by the oaks of Mamre, resting in the doorway of this tent during the heat of the day. Three men appear to him, and he immediately rushes to provide them with sustenance: water to wash up, bread, curds, wheat cakes, and choice meat to eat. As a foreigner himself, Abraham was eager to welcome other sojourners.

For he himself is our peace, who has made us both one and has broken down in his flesh the dividing wall of hostility.

EPH 2:14

Abraham thought he was entertaining men, but actually he was offering hospitality to the Lord himself. The three strangers, who are soon revealed as angelic

47. George Arthur Buttrick, ed. *The Interpreter's Dictionary of the Bible*, Volume 4 (Nashville: Abingdon Press, 1962), 399.

messengers from God, bring Abraham good news of Sarah's promised conception. Abraham's story reminds us not to let opportunities to show hospitality pass us by. "Do not neglect to show hospitality to strangers, for thereby some have entertained angels unawares," we read in Hebrews 13:2.

Other biblical examples of hospitality in a redemptive role include:

- Elijah at Zarephath: God commanded the widow to provide for him and God in return sustained their food supply (1 Kgs 17).
- Ruth in Bethlehem: Boaz ensured that Ruth and Naomi received a generous share of the harvest (Ruth 2).
- Elisha in Shunem: A Gentile woman provided food and residence for Elisha because he was a prophet of God. God blessed her with a son and her land was restored to her after she was forced to sojourn in Philistine during a famine (2 Kgs 4, 8).
- The man of Ephraim sojourning in Gibeah: The old farmer took care of all his needs (Judg 19).
- Zacchaeus, the tax collector: Jesus was passing through Jericho and invited himself to the home of Zacchaeus (Luke 19). Zaccheus repented of his fraud and repaid anyone he had wronged fourfold.
- Jesus in Samaria: After the Samaritan woman at the well believed in Jesus, the Samaritans invited Jesus to stay with them for two days (John 4).
- The Good Samaritan: He who cared for all needs of the injured man (Luke 10).
- Lydia in Philippi: After her baptism she provided for Paul and his companions on their missionary journey (Acts 16).

When we, like the examples above, welcome the stranger, we not only act out our faith, but we also minister on behalf of Christ:

> Then the King will say to those on his right, "Come, you who are blessed by my Father, inherit the kingdom prepared for you from the foundation of the world. For I was hungry and you gave me food, I was thirsty and you gave me drink, I was a stranger and you welcomed me, I was naked and you clothed me, I was sick and you visited me, I was in prison and you came to me." Then the righteous will answer him, saying, "Lord, when did we see you hungry and feed you, or thirsty and give you

drink? And when did we see you a stranger and welcome you, or naked and clothe you? And when did we see you sick or in prison and visit you?" And the King will answer them, "Truly, I say to you, as you did it to one of the least of these my brothers, you did it to me." (Matt 25:34–40)

> *What does hospitality look like in your home? In what ways can you envision yourself offering hospitality to refugees, whether inside or outside of your home?*

From hardship to hardship

No one will dispute the contributions to American society, science, education, politics, and literature made by the likes of Albert Einstein, Henry Kissinger, Madeleine Albright, Gloria Estefan, Isabel Allende, or Elie Wiesel. What some may not realize is that all these luminaries were refugees. The grit and perseverance that helped them survive their flight are the same qualities that help them thrive in their new lives.

But rebuilding is difficult. Upon arrival, refugees are thrust into rebuilding their lives in a new culture, system, and language that is usually quite distinct from their own background. Many suffer from PTSD, culture shock, and exhaustion. Many develop depression. While refugees are grateful to be resettled in the States, many feel so lost here that they would prefer to return to their camp or even to their home country. While that might seem incredulous to us, we must have empathy and patience with those who are trying to rebuild everything that was lost to them. The sense of lost identity and meaning takes a huge emotional toll.

And whoever gives one of these little ones even a cup of cold water because he is a disciple, truly, I say to you, he will be no means lose his reward.

MATT 10:42

For a minority of refugees, resettlement is still the best durable solution chosen for them. Since 1975 the US has made room for almost 3.5 million refugees, settled in 180 cities. Table 4 below shows recent refugee arrivals by state.

Table 4. Refugee Arrivals by State
Fiscal year 2016

State	Total refugees	Percentage of national total
National total	84,995	100
California	7,912	9.31
Texas	7,803	9.18
New York	5,028	5.92
Michigan	4,257	5.01
Ohio	4,194	4.93
Arizona	4,110	4.84
North Carolina	3,344	3.93
Washington (state)	3,233	3.80
Pennsylvania	3,223	3.79
Georgia	3,017	3.55

SOURCE US Department of State, Bureau of Population, Refugees, and Migration (PRM), Worldwide Refugee Admissions Processing System (WRAPS), 2016.
NOTE North Dakota settled the most refugees per capita in 2015.

One of the goals of resettlement is to help refugees become independent and self-sustaining. Refugees receive government-provided short-term cash and medical assistance. Refugees also receive case services, employment services, English as a Second Language, and civics instruction. They arrive authorized to work in the country and after one year are eligible for Lawful Permanent Resident status, aka a "green card." Five years after that, they can become US citizens.

While refugees do receive government assistance, it is barely enough to get their feet off the ground. Depending on what type of assistance program they are on, the benefits can provide up to eight months of support. While that is helpful, eight months is rarely enough time to be truly "self-sustainable."[48] Churches and welcoming citizens can stand in the gap when policy is not enough. Seminary professor Christine Pohl writes:

> Reception of refugees is one of the few places in modern politics where the explicit language of hospitality is still used. People continue to connect theological notions of sanctuary, cities of refuge, and care for aliens with the needs of today's displaced people. Christians have a vital

---

48. "Self-sustaining" is defined as having a job, even if a refugee doesn't have a car or can't speak English.

role in making sure that the needs of refugees are taken seriously by national governments. But our response must extend beyond public policy to more personal involvement in voluntary agencies, communities, churches, and homes where acts of welcome offer refuge and new life to some of the world's most vulnerable people.[49]

Refugees come to America having lost almost everything: family, friends, home, material comforts, money. But they are survivors. Refugees inspire us because they have encountered tremendous hardship with resilience and resourcefulness.

Ways to care for refugees

We're heading into the practical section of the workbook, where you will brainstorm how to get into action and extend care for refugees. Before we look at your Personal Action Plan, here's a list of ideas:

- **Get acquainted.** Identify the refugee resettlement agencies in your city and explore the volunteer opportunities they offer.
- **Prepare a warm welcome.** Collect furniture and household goods for their apartment and help them settle in when they arrive or move to their permanent housing. Prepare welcome kits of basic necessities or arrange for meals to be delivered during their first week.
- **Invite them into your home.** Offer to host a refugee family who is awaiting permanent housing. Invite them to share a meal. Friendships are formed over food, but do educate yourself about the refugee family's cultural background and do not serve foods that would be considered unclean, non-kosher, or offensive to them. Learn about their table culture and mannerisms.
- **Find their "home away from home."** Try to connect refugees with people from their countries of origin. The sense of community and familiarity of language and culture will be of great comfort.
- **Find common ground.** Activities that communicate warmth and friendship but do not require much language fluency are

---

49. Christine Pohl, *Making Room: Recovering Hospitality as a Christian Tradition* (Grand Rapids: Eerdmans, 1999), 166.

a good starting place. Play soccer, play simple card and board games, visit the playground, or cook together.

- **Take them shopping.** Accompany them to the grocery store. While you're shopping you can teach them food vocabulary and how to make good selections. Afterwards, you could show them how to cook some American dishes. Show them where to buy inexpensive household products.

- **Help prepare their children for school and new friends.** Children do not have the developed coping mechanisms of adults and may struggle to understand their situation. Most new arrivals will be concerned about their children's assimilation into a new school system and new peer circles. Registering their children for school, learning bus routes, and purchasing school supplies is a daunting task and an area where locals can provide a lot of help.

- **Teach them English.** This is possibly the most helpful tool you can give a refugee who does not already know English. Teach them slang. Introduce them to the public library and to quality television programs. If they have young children, the children will likely learn English very quickly in school, and will soon be able to help translate for their parents. However, in order for the adults to be empowered and equipped to work, it is essential they, too, master English.

- **Help them get mobile.** Teach them how to drive a car, where to buy a bike, how to ride the bus or subway, how to read a map. Mobility is important to achieving independence.

- **Be a good listener.** Refugees have stories of hardship, struggle, and loss. Many suffer from PTSD and need counseling. Be a part of the healing process by lending an ear to their stories. You may find that they inspire you.

- **Celebrate the holidays together.** Find out what holidays or holy days are special in your refugee friend's home country. Include them in American holidays.

- **Help them find a place of worship.** Finding a community of faith will provide a safety network and support system. Be sensitive to the refugees' religion, and whether they are open to your Christian faith. Do not make conversion the basis of your friendship.

- **Pray for them.** Ask God to open your heart to refugees. Ask him to bring healing to the torn-apart lives of refugees. Pray for their assimilation into a new country and culture. Pray that God would open their hearts to himself.
- **Ask them for help or advice.** You read that right. Friendship is mutual, and refugees feel respected and valued when they can offer you something back. Resist the "savior complex" and look upon your refugee friends as being capable to bless you.
- **Advocate for refugees.** Churches can speak out against restrictive policies against those who need protection the most. By lifting up a prophetic voice, Christians can nurture a moral public ethos of hospitality toward the stranger. Contact your national congressional representatives and local politicians. You can start here: http://www.whoismyrepresentative.com/.
- **Participate in Refugee Sunday.** Every year on one Sunday in June churches across the country highlight the global refugee crisis. See https://wewelcomerefugees.com/nationalrefugeesunday/.
- **Read refugee memoirs and watch refugee documentaries.** These will open your eyes to the experiences of refugees. See Appendix B and the Bibliography for ideas.
- **Most of all, be a friend**! Be available to refugees. Show the love of Christ to refugees by caring for them as friends.

Which of these ideas can you see yourself taking on? What would be the first step to turning it into an action item?

THE LEAST OF THESE

A doctrine of hospitality should inform the way we view government policies with respect to refugees. Refugees have a compelling case for hospitality and mercy. When we view the world through the lens of our narrative faith, we come to realize that we have often let patriotism override faith. God, forgive us for that. The Church in America has been blessed in many ways. We are a numerically large and materially wealthy member of the global Body of Christ, with many resources at our disposal.

But those resources are not just for us to enjoy—we have a moral obliga- tion to share with "the least of these," as unto Christ himself. Jesus said, "And whoever gives one of these little ones even a cup of cold water because he is a disciple, truly, I say to you, he will be no means lose his reward" (Matt 10:42), and "Everyone to whom much was given, of him much will be required, and from him to whom they entrusted much, they will demand the more" (Luke 12:48).

No matter where you stand on the refugee debate, it will not change the reality that refugees have come to our country. Some are thriving, some are barely surviving. Scripture commands hospitality to the stranger. We experience God through hospitality offered to strangers. This spiritual reality challenges us to view refugees not as a burden but as an asset to our communities, and to view immigration issues as also moral issues, not just economic and political ones. Churches are the largest American institution capable of providing far-reaching assistance with immigrant integration.[50] But we don't need to depend on institutions. With the world in our backyard, we have a unique opportunity to welcome the stranger. Jesus was radical. Let us be radical in the way we fulfill the hospitali- ty-driven, justice-laden mission of God.

> *Conversion to God, therefore, means a simultaneous conversion to the other persons who live with you on this earth. The farmer, the worker, the student, the prisoner, the sick, the black, the white, the weak, the strong, the oppressed and the oppressor, the patient and the one who heals, the tortured and the torturer, the boss and the flunky, not only are they people like you, but they are also called to make themselves heard and to give God a chance to be the God of all.*
>
> HENRI NOUWEN*

---

* Henri J. M. Nouwen, *With Open Hands* (Notre Dame: Ave Maria Press, 1972), 114.

50. Jenny Yang, "A Christian Perspective on Immigrant Integration," *The Review of Faith & International Affairs*, Vol. 9, Issue 1 (Spring 2011), 80.

Personal Reflection

1. How has your attitude towards or perception of refugees been affected by this study?

2. What lingering questions do you have after reading through this study? Consider doing your own research online, through the library, or through a refugee advocacy organization to find the answers. (See Appendix A.)

3. Take some time now to pray for refugees, for their protection, safety, and the rebuilding of their lives. Pray that God would move in the hearts of his people to welcome refugees with generosity, compassion, and mercy.

CONCLUSION

Once I thought to write a history
of the immigrants in America.
Then I discovered that the immi-
grants were *American history.*
OSCAR HANDLIN

At the beginning of this study, you met Mariane from Rwanda. After US approval for resettlement Mariane's family arrived in Houston in 1997. They knew no one and spoke no English, so the transition was extremely difficult. Resolved to become independent, both Mariane and her husband enrolled in school to learn English. Mariane eventually found her way into the hotel industry. She was well-received there due to the global outlook of the industry itself. She worked her way up from housekeeping, eventually landing a managerial role in accounting, where she still works today. Meanwhile her husband was able to earn his M.S. in Engineering, and he, too, was promoted to manager. Gradually the family started to find stability in their new lives.

Although she still aches for Rwanda, Mariane is able to say she feels "happy" because she can see the fruit of her trials: "What doesn't break you makes you stronger. I feel like I have found myself again." Mariane encourages recently-arrived refugees to embrace the best of what America has to offer, beginning with education. She says, "People have many freedoms here and hard work pays off. Close the door behind you and open another one. You don't have to live in between doors."

For Mariane, the hardest part about continuing her life in the United States is being without her family, most of whom still live in Rwanda. "No human being would prefer losing her beloved country and being called a 'refugee.' Everyone would definitely return home if they could, but that opportunity has not knocked at my door as of yet," she says.

Mariane visited her country in 2004 and would like to retire there someday. For now, her goal is for her family to experience the American dream. She hopes to mentor refugees and help them obtain an education and become independent, as she and her husband have been able to achieve.

"THE NEW COLOSSUS"

The Statue of Liberty is *the* iconic symbol of freedom and of the United States of America. Standing gracefully on Liberty Island in New York Harbor, she has welcomed millions of immigrants, both during the period when the site served as the nation's busiest immigrant inspection station from 1892 to 1954 and to the present day as a national monument and tourist attraction. The statue, designed by Frédéric Bartholdi, was presented as a gift from France and dedicated in 1886. The Lady represents Libertas, the Roman goddess of freedom, at whose feet lies a broken chain. Her arms bear a torch and a *tabula ansata* (a tablet evoking the concept of law) upon which is inscribed 1776, the date of the Declaration of Independence, in Roman numerals.

Originally intended to represent international republicanism, the Statue of Liberty has come to be viewed instead as the welcoming mother—the symbol of America's immigration history. So many immigrants have sailed by her that as many as 40 percent of Americans can trace their roots to Ellis Island.[51] Engraved on a plaque mounted on the statue's pedestal is the poem "The New Colossus":

> Not like the brazen giant of Greek fame,
> With conquering limbs astride from land to land;
> Here at our sea-washed, sunset gates shall stand
> A mighty woman with a torch, whose flame
> Is the imprisoned lightning, and her name
> Mother of Exiles. From her beacon-hand
> Glows worldwide welcome; her mild eyes command
> The air-bridged harbor that twin cities frame.
> "Keep, ancient lands, your storied pomp!" cries she
> With silent lips. "Give me your tired, your poor,
> Your huddled masses yearning to breathe free,
> The wretched refuse of your teeming shore.
> Send these, the homeless, tempest-tost to me,
> I lift my lamp beside the golden door!"

---

51. Mary Pipher, *The Middle of Everywhere: The World's Refugees Come to Our Town* (New York: Harcourt, Inc., 2002), xxiii.

This sonnet was penned by Jewish-American poet Emma Lazarus in 1883, so long ago, yet the words still reflect the American vision, a vision that today is being treated with contempt in so many corners of our nation. Our country was established on the backs of immigrants and refugees arriving tired, poor, and yearning to breathe free, just like those arriving on our doorstep today. They have suffered oppression and sadly, many continue to suffer it on our shores and at our doors.

Embracing refugees, the "huddled masses" in our midst, is more than an origin myth—it is our history. So much of America's relative prosperity is owed to the ingenuity and industry of our immigrant forebears. We are a "permanently unfinished nation," one whose story is changing at an ever-faster pace in increasing diversity, thanks to the globalized world we live in.[52] Refugees are members of our vast global family, sharing in the same common humanity.[53] Refugees are like you and me, citizens of the world who have hopes and dreams and want to establish a good life for their families.

America is still a great land of opportunity—but we can do better. We can be a better country for newcomers to make a new home. We can do a better job sharing our resources. We can do better at embracing the nations that have come. The "American Dream" is not just about the opportunity to become a financial success story, but to live in a land that welcomes all peoples and "glows worldwide welcome."

Holocaust survivor Elie Wiesel praised the "righteous Gentiles" who risked their lives protecting the Jewish refugees. May we who follow Christ advocate for the least of these, as he commanded. Walking with uprooted people through the process of restoring their lives is a vicarious act of grace, for we, too, were once strangers.

---

52. Carol Bohmer and Amy Shuman, *Rejecting Refugees: Political Asylum in the 21st Century* (London: Routledge, 2008), 1.

53. Todd M. Johnson and Cindy M. Wu, *Our Global Families: Christians Embracing Common Identity in a Changing World* (Grand Rapids: Baker Academic, 2009).

PRAY THIS LITANY ALOUD:

Their feet are tired and aching
Lord, have mercy on their soles

Their backs are hunched and breaking
Lord, have mercy on their souls

We see them there, but too afraid to act
Lord, have mercy on our souls

They fight and hope and pray and scrap
Lord, have mercy on their souls

They come from afar, we don't know their ways
Lord, help us to trust

We want to care, but it's hard to share
Lord, help us to give

They're made in your image, they're your children too
Lord, help us to love

We're called by faith beyond ourselves
Lord, help us to live

Lord, help us to see you in the face of
the sojourner
the wanderer
the shipwrecked
the lost boy
the widow
the orphan
the abandoned
the scorned
the displaced
THE REFUGEE

PERSONAL ACTION PLAN

He has told you, O man, what is good;
and what does the Lord require of you
but to do justice, and to love kindness,
and to walk humbly with your God?
Micah 6:8

Instead of reflection questions for the Conclusion chapter, you will develop a personal action plan. Your personal action plan will help you apply what you have learned through this study and take a first or farther step in caring for the refugees in your midst. Your action plan can include some type of activity, including preparing welcome kits for refugees, "adopting" a refugee family for the holidays, or watching a documentary with a group of friends.

Follow these steps toward creating your own action plan. You can do this individually or with your group.

1. Pray and ask God to direct your plans. Ask him to give you sensitivity and wisdom as you determine how you can best support local refugees. Express your fears about the unknowns.

2. Identify a particular refugee community or refugee agency within your city that you feel drawn to. I suggest you choose something close by to increase your chance of participation. To see what volunteer organizations are near you, enter your zip code on this handy link: https://www.whitehouse.gov/aidrefugees. Write down your notes here:

3. What type of activity do you feel would be realistic for you to take on? See Chapter 6 for ideas. Write down the activity here:

4. What is the date of your activity?

5. What supplies or provisions will you need for your action plan? Make a list here:

6. What expectations do you have of this action plan? If you have any qualms or concerns write them here:

7. Do you have long-term or short-term vision for this action plan? If this is something that can be a repeated or regular commitment, write down thoughts on how to sustain it.

8. Commit your plans, time, and service to the Lord. Serve as unto Him. Be willing to serve and care for refugees no matter what the outcome. They might not have the language skills to show you their appreciation. Pray now.

9. Challenge someone to do this study and/or get into action to care for refugees.

APPENDIX A
RESETTLEMENT AGENCIES

Nine major Voluntary Agencies (VOLAGs) that resettle refugees in the United States. Check online to see if these agencies have an office in your city.

Church World Service (CWS)
Immigration and Refugee Program
475 Riverside Drive, Suite 700
New York, NY 10115
Phone: (212) 870-2061
cwsglobal.org

Episcopal Migration Ministries (EMM)
815 Second Avenue
New York, NY 10017
Phone: (800) 334-7626
episcopalmigrationministries.org

Ethiopian Community Development Council (ECDC)
901 South Highland Street
Arlington, VA 22204
Phone: (703) 685-0510
ecdcus.org

Hebrew Immigration Aid Society (HIAS)
1300 Spring Street, Suite 500
Silver Spring, MD 20910
Phone: (301) 844-7300
hias.org

International Rescue Committee (IRC)
122 East 42nd Street
New York, NY 10168
Phone: (212) 551-3000
rescue.org

Lutheran Immigration & Refugee Service (LIRS)
700 Light Street
Baltimore, MD 21230
Phone: (410) 230-2700
lirs.org

US Committee for Refugees and Immigrants (USCRI)
2231 Crystal Drive, Suite 350
Arlington, VA 22202
Phone: (703) 310-1130
refugees.org

US Conference of Catholic Bishops/Migration and Refugee Services (USCCB/MRS)
3211 Fourth Street, NE
Washington, DC 20017
Phone: (202) 541-3352
usccb.org/mrs

World Relief
7 East Baltimore Street
Baltimore, MD 21202
Phone: (443) 451-1900
worldrelief.org

APPENDIX B
REFUGEE RESOURCE LIST

There are many good resources on the global refugee crisis. Here are a few to get you started.

THE REFUGEE CRISIS AND IMMIGRATION

Bauman, Stephan, Matthew Soerens, and Issam Smeir. *Seeking Refuge: On the Shores of the Global Refugee Crisis*. Chicago: Moody Publishers, 2016.
Chapter 5 of this informative book provides details on the resettlement process and the role of agencies. The appendix contains this link to a map showing the locations of the major resettlement agencies in the US: http://bit.ly/RefugeeResettlementMap.

Carroll R., M. Daniel. *Christians at the Border: Immigration, the Church, and the Bible*. Grand Rapids: Baker Academic, 2008.
Currently one of the foremost scholars on the subject of Christian perspectives on immigration reform, Carroll is uniquely qualified as a Hispanic and American-born citizen to speak on Christians and immigration. He explores whether immigrant influx (specifically Hispanic) should be viewed as an invasion or opportunity, and grounds his positions on biblical principles.

Castles, Stephen, and Mark J. Miller. *The Age of Migration: International Population Movements in the Modern World*. New York: The Guilford Press, 2009.
An introduction to contemporary migration, written by leading scholars in the field. The book overviews the nature of migration flows and their consequences for states and societies. It also looks at the impact of ethnic diversity on economies, cultures, and political institutions.

Loescher, Gil, Alexander Betts, and James Milner. *The United Nations High Commissioner for Refugees (UNHCR): The Politics and Practice of Refugee Protection into the Twenty-First Century.* London: Routledge, 2008. A concise and comprehensive introduction to both the world of refugees and the UN organization that protects and assists them. Written by experts in the field, it traces the relationship between state interests, global politics, and the work of the UNHCR.

Soerens, Matthew, and Jenny Hwang. *Welcoming the Stranger: Justice, Compassion & Truth in the Immigration Debate.* Downers Grove: Intervarsity Press, 2009.
Soerens and Hwang are immigration experts who work with World Relief, the humanitarian arm of the National Association of Evangelicals. Their groundbreaking book advocates for Comprehensive Immigration Reform that does not criminalize undocumented immigrants but rather facilitates their legalization process in a compassionate, sensible, and just manner.

MEMOIRS AND INSPIRATIONAL STORIES

Ahmedi, Farah with Tamim Ansary. *The Other Side of the Sky.* New York: Gallery, 2006.
An Afghan high school student's poignant memoir of her losses and gains as a refugee fnow living in the US.

Eggers, Dave. *What is the What.* New York: Vintage, 2007.
The inspiring biography of a Lost Boy of Sudan who resettles in the United States, where he finds promise but also faces challenges and heartache.

Pipher, Mary. *The Middle of Everywhere: The World's Refugees Come to Our Town.* New York: Harcourt, Inc., 2002.
Drawing upon anthropology, sociology, and psychology, Pipher offers personal and moving anecdotal portraits of the complexity of refugees' assimilation into American life.

St. John, Warren. *Outcasts United: An American Town, a Refugee Team, and One Woman's Quest to Make a Difference.* New York: Random House, 2009.
The extraordinary tale of a refugee youth soccer team and the transformation of a small American town.

HOSPITALITY

Oden, Amy G., ed. *And You Welcomed Me: A Sourcebook on Hospitality in Early Christianity*. Nashville: Abingdon Press, 2001.
A collection of early Christian texts regarding hospitality and its practices.

Pohl, Christine D. *Making Room: Recovering Hospitality as a Christian Tradition*. Grand Rapids: William B. Eerdmans Publishing Company, 1999.
The author revisits the heritage and discipline of welcoming strangers throughout church history. The book includes contemporary communities of hospitality, such as L'Abri and Jubilee Partners.

Van Opstal, Sandra Maria. *The Next Worship: Glorifying God in a Diverse World*. Chicago: Intervarsity Press, 2016.
Likening diverse worship to a sumptuous banquet, Van Opstal shows how worship leaders can set the table and welcome worshipers from every tribe and tongue.

Yong, Amos. *Hospitality & the Other: Pentecost, Christian Practices, and the Neighbor*. Maryknoll: Orbis Books, 2008.
Yong shows that the religious "other" is not a mere object for conversion but a neighbor to whom hospitality must be both extended and received. A deeply analytical book, the author builds on ancient Christian practices, as well as Pentecostal, pneumatological, and eschatological theology.

STATEMENTS ON REFUGEES

Below are official statements by various groups with regard to refugees:

World Council of Churches. *A Moment to Choose: Risking to be with Uprooted People, Statement on Uprooted People*, 1995. See also: *A Moment to Choose: Risking to be with Uprooted People, A Resource Book*, 1996.
In 1995, the World Council of Churches adopted this "Statement on Uprooted People" to address uprooted people as a major global crisis. The statement challenges churches to welcome and stand with the stranger, asserting that it is a human right to remain in one's homeland.

Great Commandment + Great Commission (CG2). "Christian Declaration on Caring for Refugees: An Evangelical Response." http://www.christianitytoday.com/edstetzer/2016/january/church -leaders-speak-on-refugees.html
Various evangelical leaders gathered at Wheaton College in December 2015 and January 2016 to craft a response to the refugee crisis. The statement is quoted here: http://www.christianitytoday.com/edstetzer/2016 /january/church-leaders-speak-on-refugees.html.

Lausanne Committee for World Evangelization, Mini-Consultation on Reaching Refugees. *No. 5 Thailand Report—Christian Witness to Refugees*, 1980.
An occasional paper drafted by the Lausanne Committee for World Evangelization emerging from the Consultation on World Evangelization held in Pattaya, Thailand in June 1980. This paper representing the collective evangelical voice presents the biblical mandate to protect refugees, and offers guidelines for responsible Christian action.

"Strangers No Longer: Together on the Journey of Hope." A Pastoral Letter Concerning Migration by Catholic Bishops of Mexico and the United States, 2003. http://www.vacatholic.org/documents/Immigrants -Strangers-No-Longer.pdf

United Nations "New York Declaration for Migrants and Refugee." Issued on September 15, 2016, at the United Nations Summit for Migrants and Refugees, September 19, 2016, in New York, NY. http://refugeesmigrants .un.org/declaration.

National Association of Evangelicals. "Open Letter on Immigration Reform." November 12, 2012. http://nae.net/open-letter-on-immigration -reform/Christians and Immigration Reform in America.

CARING FOR REFUGEES

Corbett, Steven, and Brian Fikkert. *When Helping Hurts: How to Alleviate Poverty Without Hurting the Poor . . . and Yourself*. Chicago: Moody Publishers, 2014.
This book shows how some alleviation efforts, failing to consider the complexities of poverty, have actually (and unintentionally) done more harm than good.

Kirk, Jeffrey. *10 million to 1: Refugee Resettlement—A How-to Guide.*
Bloomington: Balboa Press, 2011.
This book is helpful for those seeking to establish grassroots resettlement teams.

Mollica, Richard F. *Healing Invisible Wounds: Paths to Hope and Recovery in a Violent World.* Nashville: Vanderbilt University Press, 2008.
The director of the Harvard Program in Refugee Trauma celebrates "the capacity of persons to recover from violent events and to engage in self-healing." Passionately endorsing a humanitarian, holistic, and culturally sensitive approach to healing, Mollica persuades with pertinent reference to contemporary neuroscience and to ancient and non-Western healing practices.

EDUCATING CHILDREN ABOUT REFUGEES

Naidoo, Beverly. *Making It Home: Real-Life Stories from Children Forced to Flee.* New York: Dial Books, 2004.
A children's book of testimonies by young children refugees. Includes a brief historical introduction to each of the regions of origin of the refugees.

Tavangar, Homa Sabet. *Growing Up Global: Raising Children to Be at Home in the World.* New York: Ballantine Books, 2009.
A hands-on parenting book to help children develop global sensibilities. Filled with creative and practical tips this book could equally help adults become better global citizens.

Your Land: My Land. yourlandmyland.weebly.com.
Join children from all over the United States in welcoming our newest friends and neighbors! Create personalized cards, letters, and artwork to send to children who are settling into their first American homes.

DOCUMENTARIES

Asylum (2003)
Sandy McLeod and Gini Reticker, 20 min
Upon her father insisting that she undergo a circumcision and marry against her will, a young woman escapes Ghana for the United States. Arriving in the US with a phony passport, she was imprisoned by the INS for one year while her asylum case was tried.

Between Earth and Sky (2009)
Kalyanee Mam and David Mendez, 30 min
http://chickeneggpics.org/grantee/between-earth-sky
Torn from home and country and set adrift in a foreign world, three young Iraqis struggle to find hope as they yearn for a lost past and face a desperate and uncertain future.

Brothers and Others (2002)
Nicolas Rossier, 54 min
In interviews following the 9/11 attacks with Arab and Muslim immigrants, government representatives, and legal and historical experts, this film explores how America's fear of terrorism has negatively impacted many US residents.

God Grew Tired of Us (2006)
Christopher Dillon Quinn and Tommy Walker, 89 min
Orphaned by civil war, the "Lost Boys" of Sudan are granted asylum in the US but struggle to transition to American life.

Hamedullah: The Road Home (2012)
Sue Clayton, 23 min
The story of a young refugee in the UK who was deported back to Afghanistan.

The Journey to Europe (2016)
Matthew Cassel, six-part series
http://www.newyorker.com/news/news-desk/the-journey-from-syria
-part-one
One Syrian refugee's story to get to Europe and be reunited with his family, who eventually joins him there.

The Letter (2003)
Ziad H. Hamzeh, 76 min
In the wake of 9/11, a firestorm erupts when the mayor of Lewiston, Maine sends a letter to 1,100 newly arrived Somali refugees advising that the city's resources are strained to the limit and requesting that other Somalis not move to the city. Interpreted as racism by some and a rallying cry by white supremacist groups across the US, *The Letter* documents the crossfire of emotions and events.

A Life on Hold (2012)
Nick Francis and Marc Silver, 7 min
https://vimeo.com/36908352
Produced by Amnesty International, the film is an intimate portrait of Omar, a 17-year old stranded in a refugee camp since the 2011 war in Libya.

Lost Boys of Sudan (2004)
Megan Mylan and Jon Shenk, 87 min
A feature-length documentary that follows two Sudanese refugees from Sudan and Kenya to the US. Winner of an Independent Spirit Award and two Emmy nominations.

North Korea—Shadows and Whispers (2000)
Kim Jung-Eun, 52 min
https://www.journeyman.tv/film/864
This documentary, filmed in the remote northeast mountains of China, captures the dire circumstances of North Korean refugees who journey to China.

Moving to Mars (2009)
Mat Whitecross, 90 min
The epic journey made by two Burmese families from a vast refugee camp on the Thai/Burma border to their new homes in the UK.

Rain is Beautiful (2012)
Nick Francis and Marc Silver, 8 min
https://vimeo.com/47612730
A follow up to "A Life On Hold," "Rain is Beautiful" begins with emotional farewells at the camp as Omar leaves his friends behind to begin a new life in Sandviken, in northern Sweden.

Roosevelt's America (2004)
Roger Weisberg and Tod Lending, 30 min
The inspirational story of a Liberian refugee who resettles in Chicago and his attempts to reunite with his wife and young daughter, who are still in Liberia. Winner of numerous awards at the Columbus International Film and Video Festival, the San Francisco Black Film Festival, the Cleveland Film Festival, and other venues.

Salam Neighbor (2016)
Zach Ingrasci and Chris Temple, 75 min
http://livingonone.org/salamneighbor/
Two Americans spent one month living inside Za'atari refugee camp among thousands of Syrian refugees.

The Split Horn: Life of a Hmong Shaman in America (2001)
Taggart Siegel, 60 min
https://vimeo.com/47612730
The emotional saga of a Hmong shaman and his family who were transplanted from the mountains of Laos during the Vietnam War to America's heartland. This intimate family portrait explores universal issues of cultural transformation, spirituality, and family.

The Stranger (2014)
Linda Midgett, 40 min
Commissioned by the Evangelical Immigration Table, this film profiles three immigrant stories and includes interviews with Christian leaders.

Then I Came by Boat (2014)
Marleena Forward, 13 min
http://www.imdb.com/title/tt4292458/
In this award-winning short documentary, Tri Nguyen shares his memories of leaving war-torn Vietnam as a child to cross the ocean on a wooden boat, and then being received as a refugee in Australia.

The Trials of Jacob Mach (2013)
New York Times Documentary, 23 min
A documentary follows a Lost Boy who, 12 years after leaving Sudan, has found that the dream of a better life is both all around and just outside his grasp.

Two at the Border (2013)
Tuna Kaptan and Felicitas Sonvilla, 30 min
http://thoseattheborder.com/englisch-2.html
A portrait of two human smugglers from Syria and Palestine at the border between Turkey and Greece.

The Unreturned (2008)
Nathan Fisher, 75 min
Filmed in Syria and Jordan, this documentary analyzes Iraq's continuing middle class refugee disaster through the eyes of five displaced Iraqis.

REFUGEE ADVOCACY AND ASSISTANCE ORGANIZATIONS

American Refugee Committee

arcrelief.org

An international nonprofit, nonsectarian organization that has provided humanitarian assistance and training to millions of beneficiaries over the last 30 years, ARC provides shelter, clean water and sanitation, health care, skills training, microcredit education, and protection.

Boat People SOS

bpsos.org

Established in 1980 to assist Vietnamese "Boat People" in the aftermath of the Vietnam War, BPSOS exists "to transform victims into survivors and active citizens who reach out and help others like them achieve liberty and dignity."

Christian Community Development Association

ccda.org

Many of its member organizations serve immigrants and refugees. See website for a directory.

Christians for Comprehensive Immigration Reform

faithandimmigration.org

A campaign of sojourners, CCIR is a coalition of Christian organizations, churches, and leaders from across the US theological and political spectrum, united in support of Comprehensive Immigration Reform.

Evangelical Immigration Table

evangelicalimmigrationtable.com

"Preaching God's Heart for Immigrants." Take the "I Was a Stranger" challenge: http://evangelicalimmigrationtable.com/iwasastranger/.

I Am a Migrant/I am a Refugee

RefugeesMigrants.Org

Explore personal stories of migrants and refugees on this website powered by the International Organization for Migration..

Institute for Global Engagement

globalengage.org

IGE works at the critical intersection of religion and global affairs, building sustainable environments for religious freedom worldwide. Their Center on Faith and International Affairs publishes the quarterly *Review of Faith & International Affairs*, the only journal of its kind on religion in global affairs.

Internal Displacement Monitoring Centre

internal-displacement.org

Established in 1998 by the Norwegian Refugee Council (NRC), IDMC is the leading international body monitoring conflict-induced internal displacement worldwide.

International Committee of the Red Cross

icrc.org

The ICRC is an independent, neutral organization whose exclusively humanitarian mission is to protect the lives and dignity of victims of armed conflict and other situations of violence.

International Organization for Migration

iom.int

The leading international organization on migration, the IOM is the UN's migration agency, committed to the principle that humane and orderly migration benefits migrants and society.

Office of Refugee Resettlement (US Department of Health and Human Services)

acf.hhs.gov/orr

Founded on the belief that newly arriving populations have inherent capabilities when given opportunities, the ORR provides people in need with critical resources to assist them in becoming integrated members of American society.

Refugee Council USA

rcusa.org

A coalition of 22 US-based non-governmental organizations, dedicated to refugee protection, welcome, and excellence in the US refugee resettlement program.

Refugees International

refugeesinternational.org

Refugees International advocates for lifesaving assistance and protection for displaced people and promotes solutions to displacement crises.

RefugePoint

Refugepoint.org

RefugePoint provides lasting solutions for the world's most at-risk refugees. We identify and protect refugees who have fallen through the cracks of humanitarian assistance and have no other options for survival, in particular women, children, and urban refugees.

Refugee Processing Center

wrapsnet.org

The Refugee Processing Center is the creator of WRAPS, a customized computer software system to assist the processing of refugees bound for resettlement in the United States. This website provides State Department reports on refugee arrivals.

Refugee Studies Centre

rsc.ox.ac.uk

The leading multidisciplinary centre for research and teaching on the causes and consequences of forced migration, combining world-class academic research with a commitment to improving the lives and situations for some of the world's most disadvantaged people.

Sojourners

sojo.net

Social justice journalism whose mission is "to articulate the biblical call to social justice, inspiring hope and building a movement to transform individuals, communities, the church, and the world."

The United Methodist Committee on Relief

umcor.org

UMCOR is dedicated to alleviating human suffering around the globe. UMCOR's work includes programs and projects in disaster response, health, sustainable agriculture, food security, relief supplies, and more.

The United Nations High Commission for Refugees (UNHCR)

unhcr.org

This UN agency is mandated to lead and coordinate international action to protect refugees and resolve refugee problems worldwide. Its primary purpose is to safeguard the rights and well-being of refugees. UNHCR strives to ensure that everyone can exercise the right to seek asylum and find safe refuge in another State, with the option to return home voluntarily, integrate locally, or to resettle in a third country. It also has a mandate to help stateless people.

Urban Refugees

Urban-refugees.org

Urban Refugees is a not-for-profit organization dedicated to improving the lives of urban refugees and internally displaced persons in developing countries.

World Relief

wr.org

One of the nine major VOLAGs, World Relief is the humanitarian arm of the National Association of Evangelicals, their mission is: "Empowering the local Church to serve the most vulnerable." World Relief has published a wonderful learning group document called "Welcoming the Stranger." You can download it for free: http://welcomingthestranger.com/.

Women's Refugee Commission

womensrefugeecommission.org

WRC lead the international community's work to protect and empower refugee women and girls. They ensure women's right to sexual and reproductive health care, to safety from gender-based violence, and to economic and social empowerment.

APPENDIX C
INCREASING YOUR CULTURAL INTELLIGENCE (CQ)

In today's globalized world it is hard to get by without understanding diverse cultures and communication styles. Caring for refugees requires cultural sensitivity and intelligence. Below are a few ideas to help you and your family raise your Cultural Intelligence (CQ).

Know the countries of the world.
How many of the world's 196 countries can you correctly identify on a map? Print out the outline maps on this educational website: www.eduplace.com/ ss/maps/. Then grab an atlas and give it a try!

Watch international movies and listen to international music.
Get a taste of foreign pop culture. Find out who the big stars are in other countries.

Read international memoirs.
Memoirs give insight and a personal touch to historical events, what otherwise might be just impersonal facts.

Learn a new language.
Not only will you gain a useful skill that will help you communicate with newly-arrived immigrants, but you will also experience the frustrations that come along with learning a new language, thus helping you empathize with first-time English learners.

Try new foods.
Visit an ethnic grocery store or a restaurant in an ethnic neighborhood. Broaden your palate, since hospitality and meal-sharing are such a vital part of building friendships.

RECOMMENDED

Cultural Intelligence Center: culturalq.com.

Gerzon, Mark. *American Citizen, Global Citizen*. Boulder: Spirit Scope Publishing, 2010.

Livermore, David. *Cultural intelligence: Improving Your CQ to Engage Our Multicultural World*. Grand Rapids: Baker Academic, 2009.

Martin, Jamie C. *Give Your Child the World: Raising Globally Minded Kids One Book at a Time*. Grand Rapids: Zondervan, 2016.

Tavangar, Homa Sabet. *Growing Up Global: Raising Children to Be at Home in the World*. New York: Ballantine Books, 2009.

APPENDIX D
THE REFUGEE EXPERIENCE

A great way to develop empathy for refugees is to put yourself in the shoes of a "stranger" for a day.

REFUGEE SIMULATION

Several organizations have created simulations or games to give you a glimpse into what refugees have to face. Here are a handful that vary in complexity and length:

- Office of the High Commissioner for Refugees (UNHCR): http://www.unhcr.org/473dc1772.pdf
- Jesuit Refugee Services: Go to jrusa.org and type in "Walk a Mile in My Shoes" in the search bar.
- Lutheran Immigration and Refugee Services (LIRS): http://lirs.org/wp-content/uploads/2014/04/LIRS-Refugee -Simulation-Game.pdf
- TEAR Australia: https://www.tear.org.au/resources /refugee-simulation-game#relatedFiles

WORLD REFUGEE DAY

In addition to participating in a simulation you could share the refugee experience with your church or community by commemorating World Refugee Day. Every year on June 20, the UNHCR organizes events around the world "to highlight the plight of refugees under our care and to advocate on their behalf for the help they need." Check to see if your city is organizing a local World Refugee Day.

The following ideas could help you promote World Refugee Day:

- Share personal stories of refugees
- Watch a documentary
- Invite a refugee to speak to your group
- Raise funds for a refugee advocacy organization

- Gather people in prayer
- Invite restaurants that serve the native cuisine of refugees in your community

For more information, visit www.unrefugees.org.

BIBLIOGRAPHY

Bohmer, Carol, and Amy Shuman. *Rejecting Refugees: Political Asylum in the 21st Century.* London: Routledge, 2008.

Bonomolo, Alessandro, and Stephanie Kirchgaessner. "UN Says 800 Migrants Dead in Boat Disaster as Italy Launches Rescue of Two More Vessels." *The Guardian,* April 20, 2015, https://www.theguardian.com/world/2015/apr/20/italy-pm-matteo-renzi-migrant-shipwreck-crisis-srebrenica-massacre (accessed October 24, 2016).

Buttrick, George Arthur, ed. *The Interpreter's Dictionary of the Bible,* Volume 4. Nashville: Abingdon Press, 1962.

Cambodian Mutual Assistance Association. "About Us," http://www.cmaalowell.org/wp/?page_id=7 (accessed October 20, 2016).

Chacour, Elias with David Hazard. *Blood Brothers: The Dramatic Story of a Palestinian Christian Working for Peace in Israel.* Grand Rapids: Chosen Books, 2003.

Davenport, Carol, and Campbell Robertson. "Resettling the First 'Climate Refugees.'" *New York Times,* May 3, 2016, http://www.nytimes.com/2016/05/03/us/resettling-the-first-american-climate-refugees.html (accessed October 22, 2016).

De Pillis, Lydia, Kulwant Saluja, and Denise Lu. "A Visual Guide to 75 Years of Major Refugee Crises Around the World." *Washington Post,* December 21, 2015, https://www.washingtonpost.com/graphics/world/historical-migrant-crisis/ (accessed October 16, 2016).

Donahue, Patrick, and Arne Delfs. "Germany Saw 1.1 Million Migrants in 2015 as Debate Intensifies." *Bloomberg,* January 6, 2016, https://www.bloomberg.com/news/articles/2016-01-06/germany-says-about-1-1-million-asylum-seekers-arrived-in-2015 (accessed December 12, 2016).

Donico, Mary Yu, ed. *Asian American Society: An Encyclopedia.* "Cambodian Americans." Thousand Oaks: SAGE Publications, Inc., 2014.

Engel, Pamela. "Trump on Syrian refugees: 'Lock Your Doors, Folks.'" *Business Insider,* April 25, 2016, http://www.businessinsider.com/trump-syrian-refugees-isis-2016-4 (accessed October 26, 2016).

Forché, Carolyn. "The Boatman." *Poetry,* October 2016.

Ghoshal, Animesh, and Thomas M. Crowley. "Refugees and Immigrants: A Human Rights Dilemma." *Human Rights Quarterly,* Vol. 5, No. 3 (August 1983).

Gjelten, Tom, and Marisa Peñaloza. "Built by Immigrants, US Catholic Churches Bolstered by Them Once Again." National Public Radio, September 9, 2015, http://www.npr.org/2015/09/09/437219447 /built-by-immigrants-u-s-catholic-churches-bolstered-by-them -once-again (accessed October 23, 2016).

Great Commandment + Great Commission Summit on the Church and Refugees (GC2 Summit). "Christian Declaration on Caring for Refugees: An Evangelical Response," http://www.gc2summit .com/statement/ (accessed November 20, 2016, inactive). See also http://www.christianitytoday.com/edstetzer/2016/january/church -leaders-speak-on-refugees.html (accessed November 20, 2016).

Internal Displacement Monitoring Center. "Global Estimates 2015: People Displaced by Disasters." July 2015, p. 8, http://www .internal-displacement.org/assets/library/Media/201507 -globalEstimates-2015/20150713-global-estimates-2015-en-v1 .pdf (accessed December 1, 2016).

International Organization for Migration. "United States of America." https://www.iom.int/countries/united-states-america   (accessed October 22, 2016).

Johnson, Todd M. "USA Evangelicals/Evangelicals in a Global Context." *Lausanne World Pulse,* January 2006, http:// www.lausanneworldpulse.com/research-php/196/01-2006 (accessed September 29, 2016).

Johnson, Todd M., and Cindy M. Wu. *Our Global Families: Christians Embracing Common Identity in a Changing World.* Grand Rapids: Baker Academic, 2009.

Kingsley, Patrick. "More than 700 Migrants Feared Dead in Mediterranean Sinkings." *The Guardian,* May 29, 2016, https://www. theguardian.com/world/2016/may/29/700-migrants-feared-dead -mediterranean-says-un-refugees (accessed October 24, 2016).

Lee, Morgan. "Here's Where America's 338,000 Christian Refugees Come From." *Christianity Today,* November 20, 2015, http://www .christianitytoday.com/gleanings/2015/november/heres-where -americas-338000-christian-refugees-have-come.html (accessed October 1, 2016).

Loescher, Gil. *Beyond Charity: International Cooperation and the Global Refugee Crisis*. New York: Oxford University Press, 1993.

Missing Migrants Project. "Mediterranean." https://missingmigrants.iom .int/mediterranean (accessed October 26, 2016).

Mounce, William D., ed. *Mounce's Complete Expository Dictionary of Old & New Testament Words*. Grand Rapids: Zondervan, 2006.

Mylan, Megan and Jon Shenk, "Lost Boys of Sudan." 2004, 87 min, http:// www.lostboysfilm.com/.

Naidoo, Beverly. *Making It Home: Real-Life Stories from Children Forced to Flee*. New York: Dial Books, 2004.

National Archives Foundation. "Refugee Act of 1980." https://www .archivesfoundation.org/documents/refugee-act-1980.

Nouwen, Henri J. M. *With Open Hands*. Notre Dame: Ave Maria Press, 1972.

Office of the United Nations High Commissioner for Refugees. *The State of the World's Refugees: Human Displacement in the New Millenium*. Oxford: Oxford University Press, 2006.

Pipher, Mary. *The Middle of Everywhere: The World's Refugees Come to Our Town*. New York: Harcourt, Inc., 2002.

Pohl, Christine *Making Room: Recovering Hospitality as a Christian Tradition*. Grand Rapids: Eerdmans, 1999.

Refugee Processing Center. http://www.wrapsnet.org.

Sacks, Jonathan. "Mishpatim (5768)—Loving the Stranger," February 8, 2008, http://www.rabbisacks.org/covenant-conversation-5768 -mishpatim-loving-the-stranger (accessed October 23, 2016).

Soerens, Matthew, and Jenny Hwang. *Welcoming the Stranger: Justice, Compassion and Truth in the Immigration Debate*. Downers Grove: Intervarsity Press, 2009.

United Nations High Commissioner for Refugees. *Global Trends: Forced Displacement in 2015*. http://www.unhcr.org/576408cd7.pdf (accessed October 1, 2016).

———. "Life in Limbo: Inside the World's 10 Largest Refugee Camps." http://storymaps.esri.com/stories/2016/refugee-camps/ (accessed December 8, 2016).

———. "Solutions." http://www.unhcr.org/en-us/solutions.html (accessed October 1, 2016).

———. "UNHCR Resettlement Handbook." Geneva: UNHCR, 2011. http://www.unhcr.org/46f7c0ee2.pdf (accessed October 10, 2016).

University of Massachusetts Boston Institute for Asian American Studies. "Population of Asian Americans in Selected Cities and Towns in Massachusetts." https://www.umb.edu/iaas/census/2010/population_of_asian_americans_cities_towns_in_ma (accessed October 20, 2016).

UrbanRefugees.org. http://www.urban-refugees.org (accessed December 12, 2016).

US Committee for Immigration and Refugees. http://refugees.org/explore-the-issues/refugees-facts/(accessed October 16, 2016).

———. "Security Screening of Refugees Admitted to the United States." http://refugees.org/wp-content/uploads/2015/12/USCRI-Security-Screening-Process-5.16.16.pdf (accessed November 20, 2016).

US Department of State Refugee Processing Center. Interactive Reports, Refugee Arrivals for fiscal year 2016. http://ireports.wrapsnet.org (accessed April 6, 2017).

Yang, Jenny. "A Christian Perspective on Immigrant Integration." *The Review of Faith & International Affairs*, Vol. 9, Issue 1, Spring 2011.

Zong, Jie, and Jeanne Batalova. "Refugees and Asylees in the United States." Migration Policy Institute, October 28, 2015, http://www.migrationpolicy.org/article/refugees-and-asylees-united-states#Admissions Process (accessed October 22, 2016).